PLANTHROPOLOGY

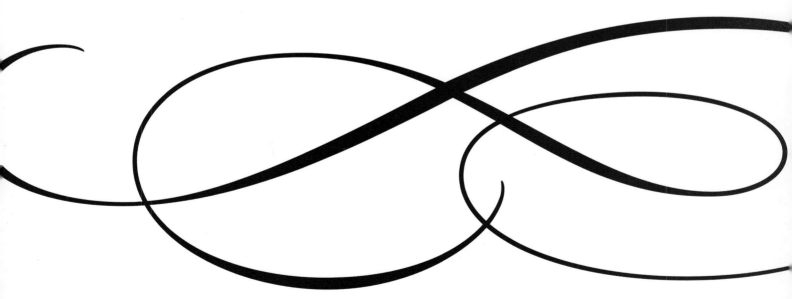

PLANTHROPOLOGY

THE MYTHS, MYSTERIES, AND MIRACLES OF MY GARDEN FAVORITES

KEN DRUSE

Clarkson Potter/Publishers
New York

COPYRIGHT © 2008 BY KEN DRUSE

A list of photography credits appears on page 283.

All rights reserved.
Published in the United States by CLARKSON POTTER/PUBLISHERS,
an imprint of the Crown Publishing Group, a division of Random House,
Inc., New York.
www.crownpublishing.com
www.clarksonpotter.com

Clarkson N. Potter is a trademark and Potter and colophon are registered
trademarks of Random House, Inc.

Library of Congress Cataloging-in-Publication Data
Druse, Kenneth.
Planthropology / Ken Druse. — 1st ed.
1. Gardening.   2. Gardens.   I. Title.
SB455.D78   2008
635—dc22   2007027968

ISBN 978-1-4000-9783-8

Printed in China

DESIGN BY JENNIFER K. BEAL DAVIS

10 9 8 7 6 5 4 3 2 1

First Edition

PRECEDING PAGE: Single-flowered *Gardenia* 'Fragrant Star'.
THIS PAGE: *Papaver somniferum.*

Louis, George, Peter, Vicki,
Adam, Helen, Lindsay, Jenny,
Jane, Mark, Jill, Jody, Chris,
Bobbi, Tom, Amy, Marcia, Judy,
Nancy, Ashley, Kathy, Joan,
and Michael

Thank you for your inspiration, devotion,
commiseration, and collaboration

CONTENTS

OPPOSITE: *Podophyllum hexandrum.*

INTRODUCTION

As a garden writer and lecturer, I travel the country doing what I love best: talking about plants with people who are as crazy about them as I am. We share stories of our trials, tribulations, and triumphant achievements, and quite often I am asked for advice, or some piece of garden wisdom. But the question I am asked most—"What is your favorite plant?"—is the hardest to answer. My best response is often "You mean today?"

Choosing one plant above all others is incredibly difficult; there are far too many from which to choose. When I stand in the garden admiring a plant that is blooming its head off, it is definitely my favorite, until I turn around and see another one doing its own particularly magnificent thing.

If I really *had* to answer, I might say the plants I like best tend to be those that have an added dimension—a little something extra. There might be a plant that is special because it looks good in all seasons, presenting flowers in summer, leaf color in autumn, shaggy bark or berries in winter, and chartreuse new growth in spring. Or a plant could be a favorite just for being independent and undemanding. But when I think of it, what draws me to these plants is one thing they all have in common: an extraordinary life story.

I am not exaggerating when I say that all the plants have tales to tell, and many of these stories are beyond sensational. For instance, there is a plant that a war was fought over, one that led to the collapse of a European superpower, and another that was used to dispatch enemies without a trace. With every new plant I meet, or old plant I rediscover, I want to find out as much as I can about its fascinating past: Who first saw the plant in the wild? Who collected it and introduced it to the world of horticulture? I am interested to find out why one plant is called sweet alyssum for its fragrance, and another "corpse flower." Which insects pollinate the sweet-smelling blossoms, and which visit the putrid ones? I wonder how the seeds get dispersed, through the gut of an animal or with built-in wings and wind?

All plants hold mysteries that may help them thrive, and there are even more remarkable secrets to discover. For example, there are geometric equations hidden within the promise of a flower bud. There are opposing arcs made by the rows of woodlike scales on a pinecone.

PRECEDING PAGE, CLOCKWISE FROM TOP LEFT: Every plant has a story to tell, an extra dimension, a tale of discovery, a medicinal use, symbiotic relationships, curious or extraordinary beauty in new shoots, fruits, or buds. Cases in point: prairie smoke (*Geum triflorum*) flower buds; squash fruit; American beautyberry (*Callicarpa americana*); early spring fern crosiers; *Asclepias* (milkweed) *physocarpa* (bladdery or balloon-like fruit); new growth of *Syneilesis aconitifolia* (rabbit or shredded umbrella plant); winged fruit of the native woodland shrub bladder pod (*Staphylea trifolia*); black asparagus-like new shoots of Baptisia 'Purple Smoke'.

PRECEDING PAGE, CENTER: Fading flower and developing seed pod of a double lotus (*Nelumbo nucifera*) variety.

OPPOSITE: How can anyone not revere these majestic "juvenile" specimens of coast redwood (*Sequoia sempervirens*)–the largest and among the longest-lived beings on earth? (For scale, that's me at the lower right.)

Even the arrangement of leaves spiraling up a plant stem presents a numerical ratio that appears in nearly all plants. The bio-mathematical formula at work in the garden is the same geometry found in the art and architecture of the ancient Greeks who considered the same numerical ratio to be the perfectly pleasing proportion. Later, Renaissance artists applied this geometry in their work. The same equation dictates the swirls at the tips of your fingers and the arrangement of the stars in the Milky Way.

Nature's art is easy to see, and artists and artisans still, as they have for ages, depict plants in paintings and use them for garden designs or as motifs for decoration. In the mid-19th century, a group of artists moved to break down the class distinctions that kept art from being available to all people. I feel a kinship with these artists who believed that beauty and nature could be the salve to treat the wounds inflicted by the Industrial Revolution; today, the injury is being caused by the industrialization of the planet.

Needless to say, I cannot turn back the clock to a time when the land I love in New Jersey was covered with indigenous tree species and woodland wildflowers. I cannot wish away my computer or my camera. Everyone is being pulled and pushed by the demands of modern life. There are so many things calling us away from the garden, which is paradoxically the one place that offers a truly restorative, peaceful retreat. I think one answer for people my age, and for young busy families, is not to necessarily shrink the garden but instead to choose which tasks you like to do, and rely on more self-sufficient shrubs, perennials, and trees for other parts of the landscape.

I've collected some self-reliant plants that I think of as stalwarts because they can compete with weeds, do not need pruning but take it well, do not demand extra watering once established, and are resistant to pests and diseases. These plants—many of which are overlooked old-fashioned deciduous flowering shrubs, or familiar varieties that have been neglected by growers and marketers pushing "new and improved" specimens—are just waiting to have their flowers enjoyed by new generations.

Nature's gifts of beauty and fragrance may be free, but I think it's long past payback time. For example, I've always felt strongly about trees, but now that more and more of them are being cut down to make way for development, I feel I need to take stronger action. I've begun planting young trees to absorb carbon dioxide and store it—doing my part to help slow global warming and preserve our natural landscape. I will not live long enough to see most of the trees I've planted mature, though I am not planting them for my benefit, alone, but for the future of our planet, and the generations to come.

One autumn, I visited The Garden in the Woods, the home of the New England Wild Flower Society, located in Framingham, Massachusetts. A group of third graders were being led on a tour. Unlike so many children's programs where nature is rendered in colorful plastic models, the tour at the garden consisted of being outside among the trees. I overheard a discussion among the children. One said, "I think it's a maple." Another disagreed. "No, the leaves are all wrong," she said,

thumbing through the guide she carried. "*Fagus grandifolia*," the girl read aloud. A third child chimed in, "Look at the smooth gray bark; it's a beech."

An ancient Chinese saying goes, "The beginning of knowledge is knowing things by their right names." Learning the names of plants—eventually, their scientific Latin names—is key. The garden is a bit like a grade-school classroom on the first day: When the children begin to be recognized by name, the teacher connects with each one, and discovers what he or she needs. The kids become people. Knowing the words in a plant's name leads to an almost intuitive understanding of its requirements. Like the kids in the classroom, plants thrive.

In exploring the stories of plants, and encouraging others to share in this exploration, I've found myself wishing there were a word or phrase to describe this study of plants and their particular histories. The *anthropology of plants* comes close, although *anthropology* refers to humans, not plants or animals. If I might borrow from this term and coin one from a green point of view, I might call the study *Planthropology*. Learning a plant's life story to know it as an individual, a living, "breathing" entity, can contribute to the success of an aspiring and even a seasoned gardener.

In this work I've explored the stories of some of the plants I love—mostly those I have known and grown through gardens in my childhood, a college dorm filled with houseplants, a rooftop in the SoHo neighborhood of Manhattan, a brownstone backyard in Brooklyn, and now, on a one-and-a-half-acre island in the northwest corner of New Jersey. Just walking through the garden, I can stop by almost any plant and summon its individual narrative. For example, the common annual rosy periwinkle (*Catharanthus roseus*) not only brightens gardens, it is also the source of cancer-fighting medicines, including one that increases survival rates in childhood leukemia by up to 95 percent. The dove tree (*Davidia involucrata*) growing in my garden is a descendant of the legendary dove, or handkerchief, tree discovered in China by Ernest "China" Wilson in 1899. But first, he traveled a thousand miles up the Yangtze River and across mountains to find the place where he was told the elusive tree might be, only to find a stump and a cabin built from the *Davidia*'s wood.

Stories like these can captivate the most seasoned garden visitor. And to a novice, the mass of green that was all a garden could be becomes a community of individuals. Once that happens, the macro becomes the micro, and there's no going back.

Living with plants is life affirming; there is something new to see, and to learn, every single day—about nature and about life. In the end, the great discovery is that gardening is a collaboration, an alliance if you will, between people and plants. I feel lucky to be able to enjoy the rewards of heady fragrance, brilliant color, and sculptural forms, and witness nature's undaunted spirit. If I do my job, plants get a healthy life, and I get to share their amazing stories along with the bounty that unfolds through the seasons—right before my eyes.

LEFT: The crescent border at my New Jersey garden.

PART ONE

discovery

I was fortunate enough to grow up in a time when children still wandered outdoors; when turning over a rock to see what lived beneath it was not done with fear but out of curiosity. Hundreds of years ago, it was curiosity and the quest for undiscovered riches that led explorers to comb the Earth in search of new plants that might promise cures for diseases, an end to hunger, or unfathomable beauty—a pursuit modern plant hunters still undertake. I learned as a child, and know today, that the most remarkable discoveries can be made everywhere and every day—just beyond the gate that leads to the garden.

OPPOSITE: Carnivorous pitcher plant *Sarracenia* hybrid.

EXPLORATION

One of my earliest memories involves walking through the woods with my mother and happening upon a clearing where a strange creature stood in a pool of dappled light. This odd thing, half as tall as I was, looked like a little tower with a balcony covered by a striped awning. My mother carefully lifted the canopy, and a secret was revealed: there was a tiny person hiding inside! My mother explained that this was Jack, a clergyman, and the tower was his pulpit, something I am sure I didn't understand, but certainly never forgot. Peekaboo was a favorite game of mine at the time, and here was a living example: a man standing in a little tower that came right out of the floor of an enchanted forest.

There in that woodland glen, seeds were sown; I was destined to become a man who loves plants. And, with a nod to that first *Arisaema*, it turns out that it's the extraordinary plants—those with secrets to uncover—that still capture my attention. These species typically appear unassuming at first, the kind of plants you need to get up close to in order to appreciate. But on further examination, these subtle creatures often have the most enthralling tales to tell.

Such intrepid 21st-century plant explorers as Dan Hinkley, Tony Avent, Daryl Probst, and Sue and Bleddyn Wynn-Jones are nurserymen as well as adventurers. They travel the temperate world looking for captivating specimens, collect the seeds, and grow them in nurseries so that the plants may one day end up in our gardens. These adventurers' cliff-hanging exploits are frequently in defense of plants, like the *Arisaema*, and they go to great lengths to rescue and perpetuate species threatened by development. There are two North American species of *Arisaema* and more than a hundred in Asia—from Korea to the Himalayas—and with the help of modern-day plant hunters, more species may yet be discovered.

TOP: *Arisaema sikokianum* may have mottled leaves.

ABOVE: *Arisaema* species, such as this jack with a whiplash causeway for crawling pollinators, are still being found in China.

OPPOSITE: Joseph Banks found forests of *Eucalyptus regnans*—the tallest flowering plant on earth.

PRECEDING PAGE: *Arisaema fargesii.*

Plants have been collected and valued as sources of food and fragrance, and utilized as botanical curatives and in food preservation, for millennia. But in the 18th century, plant exploration became a global pursuit: plant explorers, in search of answers to questions raised by science and spurred by the need to explain the mysteries of the natural world (on the promise of financial rewards), set off across the globe, often finding danger—and adventure—along the way.

GRAND EXPECTATIONS

In August 1768, Captain James Cook and his ship HMS *Endeavour* set sail from England with a very special passenger aboard. It was the British custom in that day for well-to-do young adults to complete their educations by taking the "Grand Tour" of the European Continent, but 25-year-old Joseph Banks had greater aspirations. Banks, inspired by his correspondence with the Swedish professor Carl Linnaeus of Uppsala University, the greatest botanist of all time, was more interested in nature's creations than the accomplishments of antiquity. "My Grand Tour," Banks declared, "shall be around the globe" to study the wonders of the plant world. He paid what was considered a fortune at the time, £10,000 (equal to nearly £1 million today), for passage for himself and nine crewmen aboard the *Endeavour.* Linnaeus's star pupil, Daniel Solander, joined Banks on a trip that was to become one of the best known botanical expeditions in history.

By April 28, 1770, the *Endeavour* had traveled halfway around the world. The vessel entered a cove Cook deemed safe for anchorage, and Banks and Solander went ashore to gather specimens from the eucalyptus forests and from the marshes nearby. Banks, his naturalist comrades, and the sailors from the *Endeavour* saw so many incomparable plants during their excursions that they christened the harbor Botany Bay, the name it still has today, as the harbor of Sydney, Australia.

Back in England, botanists and horticulturists awaited reports from the *Endeavour* and news of Banks's findings. And find plants he did: 110 previously unknown genera and 1,300 species. In eight days, Banks's team had amassed one of the most expansive collections ever made.

Those of us who have cool-temperate greenhouses, care for indoor plants, grow tender perennials, or live in warm-climate zones of North America will recognize the names of many of the plants Banks came across, including the familiar houseplant Norfolk Island pine, a tree that towers to 100 feet in its homeland. Banks also noted *Cyathea* and *Dicksonia* tree ferns, and the flowering shrubs *Hebe, Leptospermum, Pittosporum,* and *Protea,* whose otherworldly flowers seem to have stepped out of an episode of *Star Trek.* Linnaeus was so impressed with Banks's discoveries that he recommended that the island continent be called Banksia after the young botanist; it was not, but a genus of 75 shrubs with spectacular bottlebrush flowers, leathery leaves, and odd woody fruits were honored with the *Banksia* name.

PRESSED INTO SERVICE

When the *Endeavour* ran aground in Java, the crewmen plugged a hole in the ship's hull with a chunk of coral. While the first concern was saving the ship for the voyage home, the main worry for Joseph Banks must have been his precious herbarium specimens—carefully pressed and dried samples of leaves and flowers. Other pieces of plants were wrapped in moistened cloth and put into metal-lined chests until the onboard artist Sydney Parkinson could draw them; there were so many specimens, Parkinson could only make sketches, along with notes on the colors to be added later. I can barely imagine how drawings and especially pressed plants could survive the conditions on a ship at sea, let alone survive unexpected disaster.

In far more comfortable surroundings, and for craft projects rather than scientific reasons, I press flowers and autumn leaves. I don't use a fancy contraption with planks of wood and blotter paper, squeezed flat by a screw-clamp or leather straps. I use a much handier contrivance: a retired phone book.

I have recycled about a dozen telephone directories for this job, and it's surprising how quickly they fill up. For instance, one hydrangea flower head yields dozens of florets. Even some thicker flowers and fleshy leaves turn out fine when pressed and weighted with a few more phone books on top; once dried, they last for years.

On a few occasions, when I've needed a flower right away for a project, I've pressed the specimen in a phone book and placed the book in the microwave on low power. I check the process frequently to see if the blossoms have dried, and proceed slowly so as not to toast the flower (or burn the phone book—or house).

I've made note cards, but lately I've turned my attention to fashioning decoupage lampshades with flowers and leaves stuck to tissue paper with artists' gloss acrylic medium. I cut panels of tissue paper and glue them to a lampshade frame with white glue. When that's dry, I trim the edges of the paper and coat the surfaces with the medium, and as it dries, the paper shrinks taut. I dab a bit of medium onto the tissue and place a flower on it, then apply more medium over the flower. When the flower is dry, I coat the inside of the shade first with gloss medium and then with matte medium to diffuse light. The final step is to apply a coat of a 50/50 mixture of gloss and matte medium on the outside, which creates the look and feel of parchment.

Over time, daylight and humidity cause flowers and leaves to fade. To me, a red leaf mellowing to tan remains beautiful through all of its transformations.

OPPOSITE, CLOCKWISE FROM TOP LEFT: Pressed herbarium specimen. Pressed-leaf lampshade. Applying acrylic medium to *Abutilon* flower. Another finished shade.

The double yellow Lady Banks has become a part of my own horticultural history. On an early May morning in 1994, dignitaries from New York City's public gardens visited the garden behind my 1873 Brooklyn brownstone to witness R. *banksiae* 'Lutea' in full bloom. She was covered with clusters of double, 1-inch, butter-colored flowers dangling like cherries. 'Lutea', like her R. *banksiae* sisters, blooms a full month before other garden varieties, and creates a spectacle with her thousands of blooms. Upon seeing my Lady Banks in all her glory, not one of the guests raved about the profusion of blossoms, or the showers of petals whenever the breeze blew. Instead, all assembled uttered the same comment: "You can't grow that."

Yet, as any of the gathered could attest, a serpentine trunk as thick as my ankle grew from the ground next to the house. Two stainless-steel cables, secured just below the roof of the four-story brownstone, were laced to the top with the grass green canes and coppery new shoots. We roughly counted the number of blossoms in a square yard, multiplied that by the square footage covered by the rose, and came up with an astounding estimate of 10,000 blossoms. Although the visitors were incredulous, they had to believe their eyes: Lady Banks was big, blooming, and definitely alive and thriving in Brooklyn.

Banksian roses are known for such lush displays, and astounding longevity. A single Lady Banks planted in 1885 in Tombstone, Arizona, climbs to this day from a trunk 12 feet in circumference and covers an 8,000-square-foot iron pipe trellis. This herculean effort has earned it a designation in *The Guinness Book of World Records* as the world's largest rose. But it wasn't the vigor of Lady Banks that the dignitaries questioned in my garden; it was her very existence.

Brooklyn lies in Zone 7 on the USDA hardiness map, which means that the average minimum temperature is supposed to range between 0 and 10 degrees F. Brooklyn is part of Long Island and is nearly surrounded by water, which helps to moderate temperatures. Add to this the pavement, stone sidewalks, and brick buildings that absorb and radiate heat, and actual average temperatures might be even milder. I have recorded temperatures a bit below zero once or twice, but the rose was on an east-facing wall and fairly protected, although it was still exposed to northeastern winter winds.

Most books list the Lady Banks rose as being hardy in Zones 8, 9, and 10, where minimum temperatures range from 10 to 40 degrees F. Several optimistic nursery catalogs say the plant will grow in USDA Zone 6 (−10 to 0 degrees F, minimum average). It is possible that R. *banksiae* might be root-hardy in Zone 6—it might be killed to the ground in a cold year and come back from the roots—but it would probably not climb four stories and flower as it did for me.

Sadly, in 2003, tragedy struck the Brooklyn garden. It had rained steadily the previous fall, and the frigid winter temperatures turned the sodden soil to solid ice. Lady Banks looked sad. The stems, which usually kept their color through the

OPPOSITE: What the thornless, climbing, double-butter-yellow-flowered Lady Banks rose lacks in scent, it more than makes up for in sheer profusion of bloom—literally thousands. The plant may be hardy to −10°F, but a safer bet is in USDA Zone 7, where the temperature rarely dips below zero.

ZONE DENIAL

Tony Avent, co-owner of Plant Delights Nursery in Raleigh, North Carolina, has a motto: "I consider every plant hardy until I have killed it myself . . . at least three times." I'm not sure I could stand that much botanical slaughter. Although no fan of global warming, I, like most gardeners, am often attracted to plants listed for warmer zones.

My New Jersey garden is a solid Zone 6: 0 to –10 degrees F annual minimum temperature. But naturally, I want to cheat the zones, defy anecdotal evidence (or even my own experience), and try a plant, or try it again. Sometimes I hope that the plant's zone listing is a misprint (the number 7 looks like a 6 if you squint *real* hard), or just plain wrong. Hardiness recommendations are usually based on the temperatures and conditions of the plants' homeland, but has the nursery or reference book actually tried a Zone 8 plant in Zone 6, or in the particular microclimate that I call my northwestern New Jersey garden? (A microclimate, I might add, that is not beneficent but in a valley where cold air sinks, and frosts come early in the fall and end late in the spring.)

Instead of heeding all advice to the contrary, and forgoing a plant like *Muhlenbergia*, a native pink-flowered grass that flourishes from southern New Jersey (Zone 7) to Florida (Zone 9), I decided to challenge the zone map and create my own Zone 7 garden.

To start, I chose the sunniest area in my mostly shady garden: a spot behind the house that served as the nursery bed when I moved here and that I now call the gravel garden.

A former owner had dumped "clean fill," the stuff most new-home owners are left with when the bulldozers leave, over this area, and it was mostly clay. Clay makes for poor drainage; the soil becomes saturated when it rains, holding moisture between its tiny particles while excluding oxygen, which can cause plants to drown. In winter, roots sleeping in clay soil cannot soak up water and move it out through their leaves as they might in summer; if the water in the soil freezes, roots may be crushed as the ice crystals expand. (In general, underwatered plants are more tolerant of cold.)

I amended the clay soil to help with the drainage problems. I incorporated 4 to 6 inches of ⅜-inch gravel and about 3 inches or so of compost into the top foot of clay soil.

CONTINUED...

OPPOSITE, CLOCKWISE FROM TOP LEFT: *Acanthus mollis* against a south-facing wall; gravel garden cheats zones; crushed rock in soil absorbs warmth; Zone 7–rated *Pyracantha* 'Golden Charmer'.

A friend built a stone wall that faces south and partially encloses the gravel garden. My hope was that it would reflect heat to plants that need it, radiate heat absorbed from the sunlight back to plants at night, and to the soil in winter.

For the most part, my experiment worked. Zone 7 yellow-fruited *Pyracantha* 'Golden Charmer' has thrived, bloomed, and berried since its first season in the gravel garden. Before I moved my *Acanthus mollis* up against the wall, the plant had limped along, producing two or three stunted leaves. Growing next to the wall, it flourished, putting out more than a dozen leaves up to 3 feet tall and staying green to November. The plant has not produced flowers yet, however.

Of course, the best way to cheat the climate is with a greenhouse, but I've been there and done that. Because a greenhouse demands more daily attention than I am willing and able to give, I'll try to be content with the extra bit of warmth I can eke out of my climate with the gravel garden. And when the *Muhlenbergia* plants come into bloom, as they have each September, with clouds of pink flowers, that little bit of zone fudging seems well worth all the effort.

Perhaps given changes in the earth's climate and temperature, I might not have bothered to go to such extremes to be able to grow USDA Zone 7 plants in USDA Zone 6. In 2002, the minimum winter temperature in the garden was −8°F. Over the next five years, the temperature did not drop below 0. I don't think I can rely on that warming, and I am not happy to have my garden experience the warming trend. Along with higher temperatures comes tree-species stress and, worst so far, weed species like Japanese stilt grass, which is the worst scourge I have experienced, and a plant that is new to my area.

ABOVE: *Muhlenbergia capillaris*, pink muhlygrass.

ABOVE: Dr. Nathaniel Ward's idea led to today's terrariums, where humidity and condensation help plants care for themselves.

RIGHT: The monarch's exquisite jade green chamber is decorated with dots of gold. A chrysalis in a jar with soil led to Ward's discovery—plants grew!

winter, turned brownish green. In the spring, only one shoot began to push new growth, and in June, that single stem gave up. My Lady Banks was dead.

Were the visiting horticulturists right? Had I gotten away with murder, so to speak, for nearly two decades? Was it the rain and ice? Botanical forensics is interesting, but no help for the deceased. Things happen. Plants die. But Lady Banks and I had a pretty good run.

THE CASE OF DR. WARD

Cheating the zones and controlling temperatures promise the chance to grow more species and varieties than the garden's climate would normally allow. Having had a greenhouse, I know that providing warmth in winter makes it possible for people who garden in cold zones to defy the seasons, for the most part, and enjoy plants from the tropical and subtropical regions of the world. My rooftop greenhouse in the downtown New York City neighborhood of SoHo had a warm-temperate climate, so it was not a sultry eyeglass-fogging environment, as one might expect. I had energy-guilt way back then and so kept the greenhouse between 40 and 50 degrees F in winter. With these comparatively warm temperatures, I was able to grow the kinds of plants Sir Joseph Banks would have seen in Australia. But keeping it warm is only one challenge of maintaining the greenhouse environment. Humidity is another. A terrarium is humid by nature, and plants such as ferns, mosses, and begonias thrive in this high-humidity environment. These miniature biospheres are like a cross between a greenhouse, an aquarium, and a ship-in-a-bottle. The ship analogy is an apt one, given the pivotal role the terrarium played in the advancement of plant exploration and discovery.

In 1829, English surgeon and amateur biologist Dr. Nathaniel Ward came across a Sphinx moth chrysalis attached to a clod of earth and placed it on the bottom of a glass jar that he covered with a tight lid so he could observe its transformation. While waiting for the metamorphosis to begin, Ward noticed that when the sun warmed the air in the jar, moisture condensed and ran down the inside of the glass to remoisten the soil at the bottom. Soon the surface of the soil turned green with plant life and he removed the chrysalis to observe the developing micro-ecosystem.

A fern and a grass, which he identified, respectively, as *Dryopteris filix-mas* and *Poa annua*, sprouted and grew. Ward was especially intrigued by this result since he had been trying to establish a fern and moss rockery in his London garden but failed—not because he was not a good plantsman but because of air pollution.

By 1829, London was the largest city in the world and in the middle of the raging Industrial Revolution. "Foggy London Town" of old Sherlock Holmes movies and popular song fame was actually smoggy; dense, polluted air from factories burning tons of coal, day and night, all year round, blanketed the city.

Ward had written a paper describing "the depressing influence of the air of large towns upon vegetation." He concluded that his plants could flourish if they could live in a protected atmosphere, like the one he'd re-created inside the jar. With this theory in mind, he set about creating little biospheres, and within these ICUs he was able to replicate conditions that would sustain plants for several months to years.

In Victorian England, and in the United States, Wardian cases, as they'd come to be called, became de rigueur decorative accessories, often ornately designed, fashioned of iron and glass, and perched on equally ornamental stands. But Ward was already on to something else. Potted plants usually did not survive conditions aboard ships for months, particularly sailing from the Southern Hemisphere to the Northern Hemisphere. Radical temperature changes, wind, salt spray, and prolonged darkness if the specimens were kept below deck took their toll. Ward

RIGHT: The object of exploration was to discover new things to exploit. There was money to be made in the newfound botanical riches. Dr. Ward's case allowed plants from the tropics to travel to Europe. Bananas were imported (pictured: *Ensete ventricosum*, red banana—a fast-growing ornamental that bears edible fruit). Explorer Robert Fortune transported 20,000 tea plants from China to India, thereby establishing an industry there.

OPPOSITE: The most fragrant tea relative is *Camellia lutchuensis*.

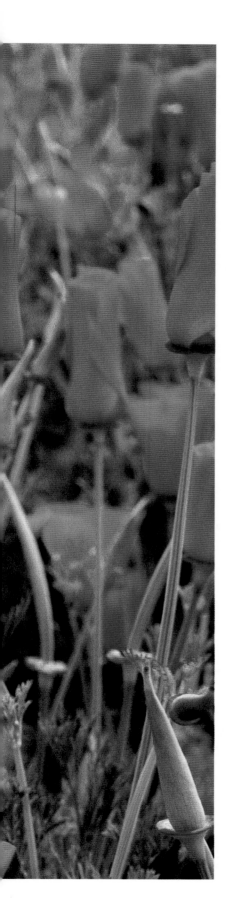

proposed that his glass cases might be a solution to the problem of "the conveyance of plants upon long voyages."

As a test, in June 1833, Ward sent cases filled with plants to Australia. The contents arrived in excellent condition. The cases were refilled with local specimens and in February 1834, summer in the Southern Hemisphere, they were sent back to England. When the ship rounded Cape Horn, the cases lashed to the deck were insulated with snow. The temperature rose to over 100 degrees F as the ship crossed the equator and fell to 40 degrees F upon landing in England. When the cases were opened, the plants were found alive and healthy—and seeds of other species had germinated in the soil.

Dr. Ward's cases revolutionized the transport of plants, and had a profound effect on the economy: Scottish plant hunter Robert Fortune transported 20,000 tea plants from China to India; banana plants from Southeast Asia and coffee plants from Africa were used to establish plantations in tropical regions of the New World; and rubber trees traveled from South America to Asia. At London's Great Exhibition of 1851, the three most popular exhibits were the McCormick reaper, the Colt repeating pistol, and a display of plant-filled Wardian cases.

NO STRANGERS TO DANGER

In *The Glory of the Scientist,* published in 1737, Linnaeus wrote: "When I consider the melancholy fate of so many of botany's [zealots], I am tempted to ask whether men are in their right mind who so desperately risk life and everything else through the love of collecting plants."

Traveling the world to see botanical wonders for the first time sounds thrilling, but plant hunting was no posy-picking party. Explorers often risked life and limb to locate a plant, sometimes losing both in the process. George Forrest nearly starved to death while being chased by Tibetan warrior priests, and on his seventh expedition, having recorded more than 1,200 plants, he died of a massive heart attack. Reginald Farrer succumbed to pneumonia in the mountains of Burma; A. Ludwig died of a rattlesnake bite in the American West; E. F. Leitner was killed by natives in the Florida Keys; William John Gill lost his life to Bedouins in the Sinai. Jon Lawson walked more than 1,000 miles through the Carolinas, with botanical riches second only to China in the temperate world, before he was captured by Tuscarora Indians and burned at the stake. Adolph Biermann, curator of the Calcutta Botanic Garden, was killed by a tiger, and James B. Chambers, a New Zealand missionary and horticulturist, was eaten by cannibals.

The search for the next new plant was more than an occupation; it was an obses-

LEFT: David Douglas found many familiar U.S. West Coast natives including the California poppy (*Eschscholzia californica*).

OPPOSITE: A California sedge meadow features meadow foam (*Limnanthes douglasii*) and Douglas iris (*Iris douglasii*).

ABOVE LEFT: The names of many explorers are found in plants, such as John Tradescant Sr.'s spiderwort (chartreuse variety *Tradescantia* 'Blue and Gold' shown).

ABOVE RIGHT: Plant discoveries continue. In the 1980s, John Fairey found an Eastern dogwood variety, *Cornus florida* var. *pringlei* (synonym *C. f.* subsp. *urbiuniana*), at 4,000 feet in the mountains of Mexico. The Zone 7 tree has flower bracts fused at their tips.

sion with botany, and a passion for adventure. Take, for example, the eventful life of Scotsman David Douglas, who traveled through North America. Great Britain has only a handful of native needle-leaved evergreens, but Douglas added dozens more to the landscape, including America's popular cut Christmas tree, the Douglas fir. He traveled at the expense of wealthy members of the Royal Horticultural Society, including Sir Joseph Banks (its founder and head for 42 years), and John Wedgwood (son of the pottery maker Josiah Wedgwood and uncle of Charles Darwin). These men subscribed to the Douglas expeditions and in turn received seed.

Covering 7,000 miles in North America between 1824 and 1827, Douglas somehow managed to escape death dozens of times. He nearly froze to death attempting to find the sugar pine tree described on an earlier expedition by his predecessor Archibald Menzies. As a passenger on a ship that sank he survived in a rowboat that was blown 70 miles out into Hudson Bay; had several serious run-ins with Native Americans; was forced to swim naked across a freezing river during a hailstorm; was nearly blinded during a sandstorm near Walla Walla in what is now Washington State (he did lose the sight in one eye, but that is another story); and was thrown from his canoe into a whirlpool on the Fraser River, losing all of his possessions, including his journal and plant collections, and spun for an hour before he managed to break free.

With all these near-death experiences, it is not surprising that he decided to head for Hawaii to recuperate, a place where he had found peace in the past. Douglas's "busman's holiday" included a climb up Mauna Kea on July 12, 1834, where he came upon a bullock—one of the naturalized cattle that roamed the island—that had fallen into a pit dug in the earth to catch the animals.

Douglas surely must have seen the exposed hole and recognized what was in it, for he had noted earlier in his journal, "The grassy flanks of the mountain abound with wild cattle, the offspring of the stock left here by Captain Vancouver." Some accounts claim that he was retracing his steps to retrieve a forgotten item and did not remember the pit, or that his curiosity might have gotten the best of him and he stepped too close to the edge and fell in. Whatever the explanation, Douglas ended up in the pit with the bullock and was trampled and gored to death. He was 35 years old.

There were suspicions at the time that it might not have been an accident. As Douglas's grave was being dug, the clergyman, as well as the carpenter who was building the coffin, noticed that Douglas's wounds were not what might have been expected from a bull's hooves and horns. His guide for the day, an ex-convict who had settled in Hawaii after serving his time in an Australian penal colony, disappeared after the incident. Douglas's large purse was gone as well. Some suspected Ned Gurney, another ex-convict from Botany Bay who had breakfasted that morning with Douglas. Gurney had also been the one to dig the bullock pit in which Douglas met his end. No one, it seems, will ever know the truth, and Douglas's fate remains one of the mysteries in the lives and deaths of plant explorers.

nippon confidential

Adventure, danger, and murder all sound romantic with the passage of time. One young explorer's journey was particularly dramatic, and could have served as source material for a Puccini opera—a botanical Madame Butterfly, perhaps. Dr. Philipp Franz Balthasar von Siebold's story begins in August 1823. As a 24-year-old German doctor and naturalist working for the Dutch, von Siebold arrived on the Japanese man-made island of Deshima, located in Nagasaki harbor.

For nearly 200 years, following the 1636 "Act of Seclusion," Japan had isolated itself from the rest of the world. During this time the Japanese had formed a rare trade agreement with the Dutch, but they were wary of all other outsiders, pronouncing death sentences upon foreign intruders. When von Siebold arrived, he and all the Dutch traders had to live on the small outpost of Deshima, which was Japan's sole connection between the mainland and the rest of the world.

Yet despite this voluntary isolation, the Japanese could not deny the benefits that came with an exchange of goods, money, and controlled exposure to modern advancements, such as discoveries being made in Western medicine. It was von Siebold's medical experience, and his name and accent—which the Japanese mistook for being those of a Hollander—that allowed him entrance to Deshima. On this tiny island, he learned to speak Japanese, and as word of his skill as a physician spread, Japanese students flocked to him to learn the latest medical practices. Von Siebold was even allowed onto the mainland, and while he refused any money

OPPOSITE, CLOCKWISE FROM TOP LEFT: Among the plants named for Dr. Philipp von Siebold is *Primula sieboldii*, a popular Japanese primrose with its own international society.

Hosta sieboldiana varieties include the ubiquitous selection 'Elegans', which has thick leaves with "good substance."

A reliable variegated selection is *H. sieboldiana* 'Frances Williams'.

Viburnum sieboldii is a large shrub or multi-stemmed small tree to 20 feet, known for its green and pinkish red fruits that ripen to blue-black.

GLASS HOUSES

Today, the relative humidity in a modern home heated during the winter months can be as low as 10 percent—equal to the Sahara desert. All plants, even cacti, find these conditions too dry. Humidifiers help, but a miniature greenhouse, a terrarium, would provide a consistently humid environment for such plants as button fern (*Pellaea rotundifolia*), *Begonia prismatocarpa*, and *Selanginella* mosses.

A terrarium becomes a naturalistic world in miniature when small rocks or stones are added. However, the closed environment is ideal not only for plant growth but also for algae, fungi, and other unwanted organisms. Avoiding disease is the challenge. I do not use potentially hazardous fungicides, but even if I did, their warning labels often list plants that will be damaged by the chemicals—the very ferns and mosses I may be trying to grow. To ward off potential disease, you must make sure everything going into the terrarium is scrupulously clean.

If you are considering incorporating natural elements, it's best to avoid driftwood and twigs, as they may harbor destructive pathogens. Nonporous stones and rocks, on the other hand, can be soaked for half an hour in a 10 percent dilution of bleach and rinsed well, or run through the sterilizing cycle of the dishwasher.

To kill any harmful organisms lurking in the soil, place your planting mix in a plastic roasting bag and zap it in the microwave for about 10 minutes on full power, or until an instant-read thermometer registers over 160 degrees F.

Next, layer the bottom of the terrarium with about 1 inch of drainage material such as

gravel, or coarse perlite if weight is a consideration. Then add ½ inch of horticultural (or aquarium) charcoal to help keep the soil "sweet" as it absorbs impurities, followed by moistened soil or a soilless medium—an organic humus-based medium works best for ferns and mosses. If the top is securely sealed, no additional

moisture will be required. Opening and closing the cases will invite disease, but dead leaves should be removed. Simply cut the leaves off with a pair of scissors, and use long tweezers to grab and remove them, leaving the terrarium open for as short a time as possible.

If this seems daunting, start small, perhaps with one humidity-loving plant, set in soil in a large uncovered jar or a clear lidless bowl with high sides. If the container is large enough—an old aquarium works well—several miniature plants in individual clean plastic pots could be gathered together on moist pebbles in the bottom. If one plant begins to suffer, it can be removed at once (pot and all), and the other plants will continue to thrive. Of course, you will have to check and occasionally water these plants in the open container.

The last terrarium I made was fashioned from a 60-gallon, perfectly sound aquarium I found by the road on trash pickup day, no doubt left there by a kid tired of his or her fish-keeping hobby. The tank has now been "repurposed" and functions very well, just like Ward's earlier versions, without the dangers encountered on a 19th-century ocean voyage.

OPPOSITE: Conservatory of Flowers (ca. 1879), San Francisco

ABOVE FROM LEFT: Layers of planting medium, charcoal, and perlite. Humidity-loving carnivorous *Nepenthes* hybrid has modified pitcher-like leaves.

ABOVE: Von Siebold named 'Otaksa', the mophead hydrangea, for his Japanese lover.

ABOVE RIGHT: *Clematis sieboldii* is a charming vine whose delicacy challenges many a good gardener.

OPPOSITE: *Magnolia sieboldii* 'Colossus' is a variety of the small tree with larger flowers that are not as pendulous as those of the species (called *Oyama*).

for his services, patients and students gave him pottery, scrolls, screens, lacquerware, books—and plants, which he then grew in a garden on the island.

As von Siebold's interest in Japanese plants grew, he employed Keiga Kawahara, an artist originally permitted to visit the island for the purpose of painting scenes of Dutch life, to paint the plants. Only Japanese servants, students, merchants, registered prostitutes, and artists like Kawahara with official permission were allowed to cross to the island and mix with foreigners.

Because of von Siebold's status and privilege, he was able to travel as a member of the Dutch embassy to Edo (now Tokyo) for an audience with the Tokugawa shogun. He collected 1,000 specimens during this trip, as well as a dangerous possession for a foreigner: a secret map of Japan. He also met Kusumoto Taki, a beautiful 18-year-old girl known by the honorific name O-taki-san. Of course, Tokugawa laws did not allow the two lovers to spend time alone together, let alone marry, so O-taki-san agreed to register as a prostitute in order to move to Deshima and live with von Siebold on the island, where, in 1827, the couple had a daughter, O-ine.

In 1828, von Siebold decided to move his family and plant collection to Holland, but before their ship could set sail, a typhoon struck Deshima. Von Siebold survived the storm, but as the cargo of the stranded ship was sorted and searched, the secret map was found and he was imprisoned. A year later, he was forced to make a choice: take his plants and leave, alone, or be put to death. In December 1829, von Siebold set sail for Java, taking with him 1,200 specimens of 485 species and varieties, but leaving his beloved O-taki-san and O-ine behind.

Von Siebold's name is not on the tip of every gardener's tongue, but the names of plants associated with him are planted in gardens all over the temperate world: *Hosta sieboldiana*, a plant that has parented many popular, bold-leaved varieties; *Primula sieboldii,* a woodland primrose with lilac, pink, or white flowers; *Magnolia sieboldii,* the Oyama magnolia, which bears the whitest of all flowers in the genus, with a ring of crimson stamens in the center of the nodding blossoms; the rare *Clematis florida* 'Sieboldii', which has creamy white flowers with a tuft of purple-black stamens; and the familiar stonecrop that might be in your garden right now, *Sedum sieboldii,* which bears succulent silver leaves edged in yellow and red.

Clearly von Siebold made many valuable contributions to the plant world with the specimens he collected during his time in Japan, but some might say that his most touching bequest is a selection of *Hydrangea macrophylla* that he named 'Otaksa' after his beloved.

THE NAME GAME

During the age of botany and the pursuit of science in the 18th and 19th centuries, the number of known species mushroomed, and there was a call for a universal system of classification, or taxonomy, that would organize plants and animals by their familial relationships. Early attempts to meet this challenge were haphazard at best; alligators, for example, were lumped with insects because they both laid eggs.

As a young student in Sweden, Carl Linnaeus traveled north across the tundra, mapping the land and its flora, and seeking new species. He returned with more than a hundred dried and pressed specimens new to Western science. But Linnaeus also considered other important aspects to plant hunting. Long before the concept of "ethnobotany" had a name, he wrote about the indigenous people he met on his travels, and carefully detailed the plants they knew, the ways in which the people used them, and the names they called them.

In 1758, Linnaeus published the tenth edition of *Systema Naturae*, in which he sorted plants by their sexual characteristics into 24 classes, subdivided into orders, genera, and species. He assigned two names to each species, defining genus first, species second. His system, known as the binomial system of classifying living organisms, is still in use today.

In Linnaeus's time, the custom was for the discoverer to suggest the generic name or species epithet. Although this system is still used today, the International Code of Nomenclature for Cultivated Plants doesn't leave anything to chance; guidelines, recommendations, and rules for naming and registering genera, species, and cultivars are presented, and plant explorers and breeders are expected to comply.

As specified in the code, species names should be descriptive, and they might tell the location or general conditions of the place where the plants are found. *Wollemia nobilis,* for instance, is a pine found by David Noble in Wollemi National Park in Australia. A plant's name may also suggest its cultural needs: *Ranunculus* means "from the place of the frogs" (*Rana*) and denotes a plant that hails from a moist habitat. Some names may describe a physical aspect of a plant, such as the color of the leaves or flowers. For example, *Campsis radicans* 'Flava' is a selection of trumpet vine with pale yellow flowers; *flava* means "pale yellow." Leaf size and shape are described by species names such as *macrophylla* (big-leaf) or *microphylla* (tiny-leaf). A plant might also be named for its resemblance to another plant: *Quercus ilex*, the holly oak, from *Ilex*, the genus of hollies, or *Hydrangea quercifolia*, the oakleaf hydrangea.

According to a 1959 directive in the code, the official scientific names for genera and species (usually in Latin or Greek) should be easy to spell and pronounce since they

RIGHT: A plant's scientific name isn't always a mystery. Horsetail is *Equisetum* (as in equine).

OPPOSITE: Oakleaf hydrangea (in autumn color) is *H. quercifolia. Quercus* is the genus name for oak, and *folia* means leaf.

are used universally. The names of cultivars—cultivated varieties selected and introduced to the market—should not be in Latin, and they should also be easy to spell and pronounce. You can judge for yourself how successful these directives have been.

The hope is that the cultivar name does not exaggerate the merits of the plant. On the other hand, the name should not be so simple that it does not distinguish the plant, nor should it be a version of the common name for the plant. And if a person's name is suggested for the plant name, the etiquette is to ask permission first.

Examples of cultivar names would be: 'Sargentii', named for the director of the Arnold Arboretum near Boston; long-blooming *Clematis* 'Betty Corning'; or *Cornus florida* 'Cherokee Sunset', a pink-flowered variegated Eastern dogwood with lemon yellow and lime green leaves that turn dark pink to red in the fall.

fruitful discovery

It had long been assumed that our hunter-gatherer ancestors abandonded their nomadic lifestyle about 10,000 years ago, when they started domesticating livestock and cultivating grasses to feed them. These grasses were also a source of grain, which provided hunter-gatherers with a new food source for themselves and brought an end to their following their food around the countryside.

Yet in 2006 a discovery was made that surprised historians and scientists alike. Carbonized figs were found by archaeobotanists in an abandoned larder in Gilgal I, a village in the Lower Jordan Valley, just 8 miles north of ancient Jericho. The site was deserted roughly 11,200 years ago, after being inhabited for some 200 years. The find was surprising because it proved humans were cultivating crops 1,000 years earlier than previously believed, and that it was not a plentiful grass crop—such as wheat, barley, rice, or corn—but a fruit that may have first sent our ancestors into the fields.

How can we be sure the figs uncovered in Gilgal I were cultivated? The figs that were found—dried as if for later consumption—were borne on a *Ficus* mutation; they were seedless, like a modern orange or grape. A seedless fruit is a reproductive cul-de-sac. In order for there to be more trees and more fruit, humans had to intervene, to propagate the plant *vegetatively*, from cuttings.

Discovering new information about our ancestors' lives and their relationships with plants is more than just an interesting addendum to the history books. Ethnobotanists continue to seek out native plants and peoples, and to learn as much as they can of the ancient wisdom from old shamans before cultures and plants disappear. What if, for example, exploration into South America revealed a curative so valuable that preserving its habitat became economically more important than destroying it? Thankfully, many countries are recognizing the potential of medicinal discoveries as well as ecotourism, and setting aside land for preservation. Perhaps exploration will once again become front-page news.

OPPOSITE: Sometimes the name of a cultivated variety tells you about the plant. *Magnolia sieboldii* 'Colossus' tells us that something is big about the plant. *Cornus* (dogwood) *florida* doesn't say much about the origin of the plant, since *florida* means "many flowers" or "floriferous." Unfortunately, the current trend is to make the cultivar name as catchy or fancy as possible, in the hope that it will sell more plants (for example, *C. florida* 'Cherokee Sunset', shown). Even though the fashion for naming a plant after a person has passed, marketers today cannot resist cashing in with a peony named 'Martha Stewart' or a rose called 'Julia Child'. I know I would be flattered.

THE GARDEN OF GOOD AND EVIL

For years I wondered why botanical gardens seemed to always have an herb display, and why these plantings—with their geometric beds arranged around a central fountain, well, or sculptural feature—were so similar. Finally, I realized that these plantings share many of the same elements because they are based on nearly identical references—historical gardens that were organized for utility and function, rather than for ornamental display. The central water feature was for close-at-hand irrigation, and the geometric beds were arranged in a specific pattern for cataloging and categorizing plants.

When plant explorers arrived in new lands, the first thing they did was investigate the indigenous flora with an eye toward their potential as medicines or edible crops. The settlers who followed gathered new plants and arranged them in organized trial gardens. Trained apothecaries studied the new plants and compared them with the "simples," the main healing herbs they already knew. The colonists also brought along their own living pharmacy of essential plants whenever possible. Some of those plants went to public physic gardens, the prototypes for today's botanical gardens, and they were planted in home gardens for emergencies as well.

Today we think of herbs as fragrant or flavorful plants used for cooking, personal care, or healing. But in the most literal sense of the word, an herb is any herbaceous plant with soft tissues as opposed to the woody growth of plants such as shrubs and trees. Whether one drops the *h* and says "erb" or "herb," as the Brits do, the colloquial meaning has taken over, but hundreds of years ago, *any* plant was considered useful until proved otherwise. In the days before refrigeration, these plants might be used to help preserve food, or to disguise the flavor when foods went "off." And before the discovery of vaccines and other modern medicines, the imperative to find cures and treatments was a powerful motivation to test plants for potential medicinal properties.

Plants were used very effectively as blood thinners, antibiotics, antivirals, and other medications, and they still are today, in low, controlled doses. In higher doses, some of these same plants can be deadly. For the most part, people stayed clear of poisonous plants, but others sought them out for that very trait. The word *toxin* comes from the Greek *toxon*, which refers to poisoned arrows. The word *intoxicated*, being sickened by a substance, has an obvious derivation. But regardless of the source and the toxic properties, the nefarious, intentional use of plants that harm has been going on for a long time, nearly as long as plants have been used for good.

PRACTICALLY ESSENTIAL, ESSENTIALLY PRACTICAL

The "formal" herb garden as we know it—artfully planted beds arranged around a central water source and surrounded by some type of walled enclosure—is one of the oldest garden designs. Ancient gardens were planted around oases that could supply water, and garden enclosures were created to provide protection from marauding animals as well as security from enemies. Ancient Roman houses faced inward toward interior courtyards that were open to the sky. In the front part of the Roman house, there was an *atrium,* which would have had a small pool to catch rainwater that was used for irrigation. At the back was a roofless, small household garden known as the *hortus.* This Roman plan was ideal for an arid climate, and it was designed for comfort: air circulated through the windows facing shaded courtyards and into rooms off the garden spaces.

Islamic gardens in urban settings were enclosed for defense as well as refuge from the elements. The central water feature often included fountains and tiled runnels leading to back gardens and small planted beds with roses, fruit trees, and palms, edged with brick or tile. These secure spaces were among the earliest ornamental-edible gardens.

In medieval Europe, when all plants were thought to be useful gifts from the heavens, herbs were grown by monks in cloistered monastery gardens. Like the Roman and Islamic gardens, these plantings were enclosed by walls and held rectangular beds radiating from a central water source so that buckets could be dipped into a well or trough and emptied onto nearby beds, or poured into simple channels for irrigation. Within the beds, tall plants were placed at the back so as not to shade shorter plants. One bed might hold a single species, or be filled with plants to flavor wine or herbs associated with childbirth.

One early plan for a Benedictine monastery included a large kitchen garden with 18 parallel rectangular beds of vegetables and culinary herbs; in a smaller area next to the infirmary were 16 beds of healing plants. The plantings were in raised beds, very much like ones we see today, with wooden sides. The beds were narrow enough so they could be accessed from all sides, and being raised, there would be not only less stooping but also less soil amendment, since fresh enriched soil could be brought in to fill them.

ABOVE: The medieval garden had a symmetrical design with raised beds arranged to radiate from a central water source for irrigation.

PRECEDING PAGE: Oriental poppy (*Papaver orientalis*)—guilty by association?

ABOVE: Islamic gardens were insulated from the outside world by being surrounded by the walls of the house. Water formed the central feature, and runnels and troughs lead to other areas, as in this plan by designer Brandon Tyson of Napa, California.

ABOVE RIGHT: Decoctions, extractions, tinctures, tonics, potions, distillations, brews, pressings, and diffusions—there are many ways to acquire the essence of an herb. For example, we make an infusion of tea (from *Camellia sinensis*) by steeping dried leaves in boiling water.

Although gardeners today may choose walls or hedges to encircle their gardens for aesthetic rather than security reasons, and follow less rigid planting schemes than did the Benedictine monks, I don't think anyone would argue that a water source in the middle of the garden, for utility as well as for beauty, just makes good sense.

outside of the box

I do not have a formal herb garden. My herbs grow pretty much around the garden, wherever they look good and do well, and I use these plants as much for their sensual delights as for their ornamental properties. I love to snap a little twig from the sweet birch trees (*Betula lenta*), sniff it, and be transported by the cherry and wintergreen smell to a summer in the country and shapely brown bottles of birch beer bobbing in a zinc tub of melting ice chunks and water. One whiff and I can practically feel the bubbles.

I'm happy to pick a mint stem from the planted pots in front of the house for my iced tea, or to shred a few leaves with scissors and sprinkle them over strawberries. I'll even dig through the snow to retrieve a sprig of thyme from the gravel garden for a January recipe.

The idea of taking herbs out of their rigid planting beds and integrating them into pretty, ornamental plantings is often attributed to the English cottage garden style of the Elizabethan era. But what we imagine to have been a familiar sight in Shakespeare's day may or may not have been. For one thing, purely ornamental gardens were the privilege of the gentry; this wouldn't change until the emergence of the middle class in the mid-19th century. For the common Elizabethan, the distinction between beautiful and purposeful was barely a consideration.

Wealthy Elizabethans, on the other hand, were enamored with their plants, and they had a particular passion for knot gardens. These were intricate arrangements of clipped silver and green herbs such as germander (*Teucrium*) and lavender cotton (*Santolina*), which were laid out in trompe l'oeil braids, loops, and ties resembling the patterned intracacies of carpets and tapestries.

French parterre gardens came soon after, influenced by knot gardens and their inspirations—the words *parquet* and *parterre* have common origins. Geometric beds on a level surface were edged in crushed rock, smooth pea gravel, or low clipped hedges. Within the edged beds, there might be paisley patterns made of one kind of plant or gravel used as a ground cover to create solid color field. The fact that parterres and knot gardens were best viewed from above is a reminder that they were made for people wealthy enough to have a second or third story, not to mention an army of gardeners to keep up with all the herb and boxwood trimming.

A DAILY DOSE

For centuries, both Eastern and Western cultures have been cooking and preserving rose hips, because of their flavor and intrinsic vitamins. While amounts vary from one type of rose to another, a single rose hip, particularly the large ones, contains substantial amounts of vitamins C, A, E, and B_1, along with calcium, phosphorus, and iron. Flavor and sweetness vary from one rose to another as well. Aficionados prefer those from *Rosa rugosa* because they are tasty and large—some nearly as big as cherry tomatoes.

If you would like to harvest rose hips from your own bushes, do not "deadhead" the faded flowers where the hips form. Also, it is critical that you not use any chemicals on the plants at any time during the year—no systemic pesticides or fungicides or any chemical sprays. *R. rugosa* is so disease resistant that it is doubtful you'll be tempted to use any "cides" on the plants anyway. Make certain that all organic products you use, including deer repellents, have been approved for use on edibles.

Rose hips are ready for harvest following the first frost, when the natural sugars are concentrated. Sampled off the bush, the fruits will be tart, and I'd advise against biting into the bitter seeds. I've sampled jelly from rose hips, but most people dry them for tea. To preserve the hips for winter, spread the washed and towel-dried fruits out on a tray or screen and place them in a cool, dry spot away from sunlight, or in a commercial dehydrator. The hips shrivel as they dry, and although not completely necessary, it is probably better to split them at this point and remove the seeds and the hairy fiber around them. When the hips are completely dry, store them in an airtight container—up to six months in the refrigerator or one year in the freezer.

At teatime, boil 2 tablespoons of dried rose hips in 1 pint of water for about ten minutes (time and amount of dried hips may have to be adjusted to taste and rose variety). Pour the brew through a sieve and into cups. Sugar brings out the flowery taste and eases the acidity. If you use honey, go easy; you don't want to overpower the delicate flavor.

OPPOSITE, CLOSEWISE FROM TOP: *Rosa rugosa* as an informal garden hedge. Fertilizing flowers. Tomato-red ripe *R. rugosa* hips. The spiny fruits of chestnut rose, *R. roxburghii.*
ABOVE: Rose hips and their jelly.

ABOVE: I like to make a wreath out of the tiny multiflora rose hips to display *indoors*. This keeps birds from spreading seeds of this noxious weed, which was imported from Japan by the U.S. government and recommended for use in hedgerows.

OPPOSITE: The flowers of easy-to-grow *Rosa rugosa* selections and hybrids are often beautiful, double, and fragrant, such as the repeat-flowering creamy-white variety 'Nova Zembla', which means "new land."

government recruited an army of volunteers to comb the countryside for the fruits. Forty tons were harvested from the prolific dog rose (*R. canina*) and the hips were then cooked up into syrup and distributed throughout the country.

The rose hips that come to mind for most Americans are probably the plump, tomato red fruits of the beach rose, *R. rugosa*. The fact that this Asian plant has bird-friendly edible fruits, and that it is not indigenous to our shores, brings me smack up against my belief about not encouraging self-sowing exotic plants. However, although *R. rugosa* can occasionally sprout in sandy soil, it is also salt tolerant and helps to fight beach erosion.

On the other hand, another Asian rose that was promoted by the U.S. government and even given away to farmers by the thousands for planting in hedgerows has become a menace in many parts of the country. This plant, *R. multiflora*, is much more successful an invader than the rugosa rose. In 2005, researchers at Cornell University released a host-specific beetle that, according to their tests, eats multiflora roses and no others—so far so good.

For now, on my property, I have been digging out the multiflora rose with mattock and pry bar. And whenever I can, I cut the berries in early December, before the birds take them. With gloved hands against the thorns, I snip off clusters and let them fall into a paper grocery bag for later use in wreaths and other indoor holiday decorations. If you can't beat them, enjoy them.

ONE BEING'S POISON IS ANOTHER'S . . .

A poison, to an animal, is any substance that interrupts a natural bodily process. In some plants, only parts are poisonous, while in others the entire plant from root to flower is toxic. Most cooks know that rhubarb stems are excellent for preserves and pie filling, but woe to the novice chef who tries to make a pie of the plant's broad leaves—they are poisonous. The toxic chemical concentrated in rhubarb leaves (and in approximately 10 percent of all plants) is called an alkaloid. Alkaloids are composed of the elements carbon, hydrogen, and nitrogen, and they taste bitter. Highly alkaline, alkaloids react with acids to form salts that interrupt normal metabolism, most often affecting the nervous system. Tiny amounts of these same alkaloids cause little or no harm; in fact, in the right amounts they actually have medicinal properties. The alkaloids also give certain desirable foods their flavors.

Caffeine, nicotine, and quinine are alkaloids, as are belladonna (atropine), cocaine, morphine, and strychnine. Less familiar are coniine (from poison hemlock) and curare, which is a muscle relaxer in low dilutions and deadly in high doses. South American tribes known for their hunting expertise dip their arrows, spears, and darts in curare (from the plants *Strychnos toxifera* and *Chondodendron tomentosum*). Curare was introduced to Western medicine in the 1940s for surgery.

Similarly, belladonna in small amounts is used for medicinal purposes, to dilate pupils or to relieve cold and flu symptoms—and in high enough doses, to dispatch a relative who has overstayed his or her welcome in a murder mystery. Cocaine, now known mostly as an illegal narcotic, was once used as an anesthetic in surgery of the eye, ear, nose, and throat—and to kill.

By now, you are probably thinking about never venturing out into the garden again. It's true that some plants make one sick if eaten, others cause a rash if touched, and several may even cause immediate and drastic results; I've heard, for example, that the first symptom of yew poisoning is death. Fortunately, we are not accustomed to casually grazing in our garden or in the wild.

Here is my admonition—Do not chew, brew, or touch the following plants without gloves (Latin names are even more important in this case, since some of the common names of harmless plants sound quite a bit like poisonous ones, and vice versa): white snakeroot, *Eupatorium rugosum*; groundsel, *Senecio* species; cocklebur, *Xanthium strumarium*; redroot pigweed, *Amaranthus retroflexus*; jimsonweed, thornapple, *Datura stramonium,* and related nightshade species; Johnson grass, *Sorghum halapense*; wild black cherry, *Prunus serotina*; English and Japanese yew, *Taxus baccata, T. cuspidata*; oleander, *Nerium oleander*; wild and cultivated lupines, bluebonnets, *Lupinus perennis,* and *L. polyphyllus*; larkspur, *Delphinium ajacis*; spurge and other *Euphorbia* species and varieties; black locust, *Robinia pseudo-acacia*; wisteria, *Wisteria* species; winterberry, *Ilex verticillata,* and other hollies; English ivy, *Hedera helix*; privet, *Ligustrum* species; vinca or periwinkle, *Vinca minor*; foxglove, *Digitalis* species; poppies and relatives, *Papaver* species, *Dicentra* species; *Rhododendron*; mountain laurel, *Kalmia latifolia*; members of the buttercup family (Ranunculaceae) such as hellebores, clematis, and monkshood, *Aconitum* species; baneberry, doll's eyes, snakeroot, *Actaea* species and *Cimicifuga* species and others; Carolina or yellow jessamine, *Gelsemium rankinji*; and the *Toxicodendron* trio—poison oak, ivy, and sumac.

Oddly enough, many of the plants listed above are eaten by animals without any drastic results. We are the only animals allergic to poison ivy, for instance, with the possible exception of other primates. Birds eat holly berries; deer eat rhododendron, ivy, yew, and mountain laurel leaves (and just about everything else), with no visible effects—except, of course, to the plants.

The idea that we live with poisonous plants may seem daunting, but bear in mind that we have lived with these plants for a long time and haven't lost a single gardener yet.

TO SLEEP, PERCHANCE TO DIE

Poppies (*Papaver somniferum*), hardy annuals with crepe-paper-like petals that dance in the breeze, are beautiful and easy to grow. The seeds of hardy annuals survive a winter outdoors, or at least most do, and the poppies are very easy to grow in poor soil, where the plants and flowers will be small, or rich moist soil, where they will

ABOVE: High doses of helpful plants can be fatal.

OPPOSITE, CLOCKWISE FROM TOP LEFT: *Taxus*, or yew, is poisonous (but also the source of a cancer treatment).

Monkshood (*Aconitum napellus*), also called wolfsbane, contains the toxic alkaloid pseudaconite.

Ivy (mature variegated shown) is also poisonous.

Castor bean is toxic if eaten (red *Ricinus communis* 'Carmencita').

Most people are allergic to poison ivy (*Toxicodendron radicans*), but few other animals are.

North American native doll's eyes (*Actaea podophylla*) can be deadly.

Black cohosh, *Cimicifuga racemosa* (*Actaea racemosa*), is also poisonous.

These threatening ornamental green fruits are of the castor bean.

OPPOSITE CENTER: The castor bean seeds are the source of lethal ricin, as well as castor oil.

ABOVE: Benignly dubbed bread-seed poppy, *Papaver somniferum* is the only genus member that contains high concentrations of a narcotic alkaloid that is the source of opium.

OPPOSITE: Other species of poppy, *Papaver orientalis*, for example, including the selection 'Patty's Plum', are relatively innocuous. But there have been reports of overzealous law enforcement officials and mistaken identities.

be tall and large. Today the plants are not that well known to gardeners, but the products made from them are infamous, including opium, a compound containing sugars; proteins; ammonia; latex; gums; plant wax; fats; sulfuric, lactic, and meconic acids; water; and more than 50 alkaloids. The modern pharmaceutical is morphine, but the poppy also provides heroin, noscapine (a cough suppressant), papaverine (used to treat blood clots and increase blood flow to the brain and heart), and codeine (which is frequently employed as a cough suppressant and analgesic).

Opium has been called upon for its various effects for thousands of years: seedpods have been found in Egyptian tombs, and both Homer and Hippocrates recorded the poppy's uses. Pliny the Elder (A.D. 23–79) wrote: "Taken in too large quantities [poppies are] productive of sleep unto death even." *Papaver* is the Greek name given to the genus, and *somniferum* is from the Latin word meaning "sleep inducing" (and the root of *insomnia*). The twin brothers Hypnos and Thanatos (Sleep and Death) are often depicted wearing crowns of poppies, and the flowers are also associated with Hymnus, the Greek god of rest and oblivion; Morpheus, the Greek god of dreams; and Somnus, the Roman god of sleep.

But in small quantities, opium was (and still is in some cultures) considered healthful. Greek athletes drank wine mixed with honey and poppy seeds for good health and strength. Doctors once prescribed it to relieve pain, diarrhea, and cough. Opium was taken orally in India for more than 1,500 years. In the 1600s, Turks ate opium for pleasure and as an aphrodisiac, disguising the bitterness with spices such as cardamom, cinnamon, nutmeg, and mace. By the beginning of the 19th century a tincture of opium, called laudanum, was a popular over-the-counter sleeping potion, recommended as a way to quiet babies.

By the 1830s, the British East India Company had become the major trafficker in opium and by association the largest crime syndicate in the world. It was illegal to import opium into China, but the British bribed the Chinese officials and traded the drug for goods and tea. The plan was clear: addict the population, and gain complete control of the market. One-quarter of all Chinese adult males became addicted, and society was in shambles.

In an attempt to stop the British gunships from bringing in more opium, Chinese junks went up against the Royal Navy in November 1839 at the port of Canton, but they did not have a chance. As a result of this First Opium War (1839–42), the Chinese emperor was forced to sign the Treaty of Nanking, which lifted restrictions on British trade. After a failed attempt to stop the British again, in the Second Opium War (1856–60), another set of treaties legalized opium and allowed missionaries to spread Christianity throughout China. In three decades, the opium trade with England more than doubled.

During the first few centuries of European settlement of North America, settlers dissolved the sap from poppies in whiskey and used the resulting mix to relieve coughs, aches, and pains. In 1874, while attempting to produce a nonaddictive form of opium, English pharmacist C. R. Alder Wright (1844–94) conducted an experiment wherein he boiled morphine and acetic acid and produced something he labeled diacetylmorphine. In 1898, after testing this product and finding it "heroic" in its treatment of pain, Bayer, the German pharmaceutical giant, launched its best-selling drug, heroin. But medical practitioners quickly realized heroin's dangers, and by the early 1900s, laws were enacted banning its use.

guilty until proved innocent

In an article appearing in the April 1997 issue of *Harper's Magazine,* author Michael Pollan warned readers not to continue reading if they wanted to grow their *Papaver somniferum,* or opium poppy plants, with impunity. Pollan reported that contrary to popular belief, growing opium poppies is illegal in the United States. He also discovered that few police officers knew this. One policeman thought all poppies were illegal, however, and declared in all of his accumulated botanical wisdom that the scarlet-orange poppies were the worst, even though it is not possible to extract opium from the plants he targeted, *P. orientalis* or Oriental poppies. After Pollan's article appeared, half a dozen gardeners around the country told me that law-enforcement officers had raided their beds, pulling up the demon plants and threatening prosecution.

It flies in the face of reason to equate a dozen poppies in a North American flower bed with hillsides in Afghanistan and elsewhere blanketed with poppies grown for opiates. In those countries, legions of workers packing razor blades are employed at harvest time, to score the ripening seedpods and scrape the oozing white latex into containers. The gummy liquid is refined in a complex process that makes turning maple sap into syrup seem like giving candy to a baby.

Quite a few poppy relatives contain some of the key ingredients in opium, but only *P. somniferum* is full of it. The poppy family (Papaveraceae) has 28 genera, including bleeding heart (*Dicentra*), *Corydalis,* plume poppy (*Macleaya*), *Meconopsis* (blue Himalayan poppy and others), *Romneya* (the California tree poppy), and some 250 individual species and varieties, among them the cold-tolerant Iceland poppy and the desert Californian poppy.

Papaver somniferum is a hardy annual, meaning that the plant sprouts, makes flowers, sets seed, and dies, all in a single growing season; and the seeds are cold tolerant, so they can survive a winter outdoors to sprout the following spring. Alternatively, gardeners can scatter the seeds in March, directly on the ground or snow. At the beginning of this century, I couldn't find *P. somniferum* seeds to buy— British purveyors stopped exporting their colorful strains and varieties—and I

RIGHT: Sow seeds of cold-hardy annual red corn poppies (*Papaver rhoeas*) in late winter. Pale salmon *P. orientalis* 'Helen Elizabeth' is a herbaceous perennial.

would have had to beg seeds from friends who continued to grow the plants and saved seeds. But one doesn't always know what one is going to get, particularly from different varieties grown in a mixture.

These hardy annuals are promiscuous. If you are happy to be surprised by what the flowers look like when they bloom, great. If you had your heart set on seeing the same ones you planted last year, you will have to intervene. For instance, if you adore the deep purple selection 'Lauren's Grape', named for Lauren Ogden, who selected it and developed the strain, it must be grown in isolation to prevent cross-pollination and to preserve the strain. If you're adventurous, however, you might try growing 'Lauren's Grape' near the red-fringed variety 'Naughty Nineties'; the resulting fringed purple poppies might be quite spectacular.

I find the pods of *P. somniferum* just as beautiful as the flowers—bluish green beneath a whitish, waxy coating, referred to as a "bloom." The pods range in size, just as the plants do, from a bit larger than a marble to the size of a bantam hen's egg depending on the richness of the soil. Each pod produces about a thousand seeds, and in order to collect them to sow for next year, it is best to harvest the pods just as they fade from blue to brown. Cut the nearly ripened pods from the plants, leaving a good length of stem attached, and carefully place them upside down in a paper bag. Tie the bag closed around the poppy stems and hang it in a cool, dry place with good air circulation. The poppy seeds will fall to the bottom of the bag as the pods ripen and dry.

The availability of *P. somniferum* seeds has increased recently, due to the defiance of gardeners and a name change. Some seed companies have taken to calling the opium poppy "bread-seed poppy." These seeds are, in fact, the very ones that crown your bagel (and fill the delicious tricornered cookie called hamantasch eaten

ABOVE, LEFT TO RIGHT: Prickly poppy (*Argemone munita*); self-sowing yellow fumitory (*Corydalis lutea*); California's large, shrubby evergreen Matilija poppy (*Romneya coulteri*).

OPPOSITE, CLOCKWISE FROM TOP LEFT: Poppy relatives include Western native bleeding heart (*Dicentra formosa*).

Spanish poppy (*Papaver rupifragum*) is biennial.

Climbing *Dicentra scandens* is another poppy cousin.

For cool summers, try *Corydalis* 'Blue Panda' partnered with grass *Hakonechloa macra* 'Aureola' and white and violet violas.

on the Jewish holiday Purim). Not too many folks have become addicted to poppy seeds; bagels, however, are another story. And, I'm afraid, the claim that eating a lot of poppy-seed bagels could produce a false positive on a drug test is not an urban myth; it turns out to be true.

true blue

The blue poppy, *Meconopsis* species, has been called the "most magnificent of flowers." With its intensely cyan to sapphire petals, it is one of those flowers that, once seen, almost everyone yearns for and yet few can grow.

French Catholic missionary Père Delavay was the first Westerner to spot the blue poppy, in China's Yunnan province in 1886, and publicize it. However, explorer Frank Kingdon-Ward, one of the most honored collectors of the 20th century, was the first to bring viable seeds back to England. Kingdon-Ward is perhaps best remembered for his romantic yet scientific writings, particularly his 1913 book, *The Land of the Blue Poppy*, based on his travels to Yunnan and Tibet. Although he believed the blue poppy was *Meconopsis speciosa*, this plant unfortunately cannot be grown away from its native habitat. Leaving the precious *M. speciosa* in its homeland, Kingdon-Ward brought back seeds of Delavay's poppy, *M. betonicifolia*, and those were germinated in England and flowered for the first time in 1926. A year later, visitors to the botanical gardens and flower shows were thrilled by the appearance of the legendary blue poppies blooming right before their eyes.

While *M. grandis,* with its clear cyan blue petals, is a species I consider particularly beautiful, *M. betonicifolia* is more highly prized. Hybrids of these two may be quite a bit easier to grow than Kingdon-Ward's species, but they still prefer conditions reminiscent of their homeland: specifically, cool, moist summers. Those of us who covet this plant are envious of gardeners in southern Alaska or Maine, and in Wales and Scotland, places where the poppies might be grown with some success.

I do not recommend trying to grow *Meconopsis* where summer days and nights are not cool—unless you want to consider installing an air conditioner outdoors. People tell me that garden writer Wayne Winterrowd, who lives in Vermont, places ice cubes on the ground around his plant on hot summer days. It may be true; Mr. Winterrowd has a reputation for defying convention, as well as going to great lengths for his plants.

In all cases, it is best to delay the flowering of a newly planted *Meconopsis* by removing all flower buds from the plant for the first two or three years. This deflowering helps the plant direct its energy into growing mature, stress-resistant roots—and thereby increases its chances for survival.

OPPOSITE, CLOCKWISE FROM LEFT: Himalayan poppies should only be tried in climates with cool summers. Rare species include *Meconopsis betonicifolia*, which is perhaps the best to try, but pinch off any flower buds in the first season.

M. betonicifolia var. 'Alba'.

One of the prettiest is the regal cyan-blue *M. grandis*.

ABOVE: *Digitalis lanata,* wooly foxglove, can be toxic like its brethren and the source of digoxin, which in small doses can be life-saving. The easy-to-grow annual or biennial can be recognized by white "tongues," each a comfortable spot for sleeping bumblebees.

OPPOSITE: The white form of the familiar English biennial is *Digitalis purpurea* 'Alba'. It is happy in a semi-shaded spot.

fox paws

In the 2006 movie *Casino Royale,* James Bond is fatally poisoned with digitalis. Yes, he dies. But thanks to the handy defibrillator in his car's glove compartment, he comes back to risk his life several dozen times, again.

Digoxin—the drug derived from *Digitalis* for centuries—is a useful heart stimulant in carefully controlled doses. But ancient Romans also employed it to dispense with an enemy, as others would a double-ought operative.

It is the beauty, and variety, of the digitalis's flowers on tall, colorful spikes that make my heart race, not its medicinal or toxic properties. I imagine golden slippers etched with sepia calligraphy, little bee-cozies, or bells running up a living steeple.

The 20-odd species in the genus *Digitalis* originate from Europe to North Africa and western Asia. The Latin name comes from the word for "finger," *digitus,* probably because the flower resembles the tip of a finger or the finger of a glove. Although folktales tell of foxes wearing "finger gloves" to keep their paws dry from dew, the common name *foxglove* is more likely a corruption of "foxes bells" from the Anglo-Saxon, *foxes-gleow*—*gleow* being the word for a musical instrument comprising a circle of bells. The German name for foxglove is *fingerhut,* which translates as "thimble," "fairy caps," and "witches' thimbles."

Unlike the hardy annual opium poppy, most foxglove species are biennial; they survive the first winter not as seeds but as baby plants with ground-hugging basal rosettes. These lush, low plants bolt in their second growing season, sending up 2- to 6-foot flower spikes by variety.

The Edwardian garden designer Gertrude Jekyll suggested planting "flocks" of *D. purpurea,* the beloved common British foxglove, on the open edge of a shady area, "to project the sight far into the wood, and to let the garden influences penetrate here and there, the better to join the one to the other." The purple-magenta species, which leans toward the light and generally produces flowers on just one side of the spike, is not my favorite, but occasionally a stalk will appear with all white flowers, *D. purpurea* f. *albiflora.* Someday, I will make an effort to root out the purple ones and try for an all-white gaggle. The color of the mature plant's flowers can be detected in the color of the seedlings' leaves. The white foxglove leaves are paler green, while the magenta plants have a red tinge to their darker foliage.

Foxgloves are best utilized as "architectural plants" in the garden: botanical exclamation points and bold graphic accents among the plantings. Larger species can be placed at the back of a border, but ones such as the 30-inch-tall *D. lutea,* which bears delicate spikes and tiny flowers, make an excellent "see-through" plant for the front of the midsummer border, although you'll need at least a dozen of these plants for any kind of a show.

When I was searching for flowers and foliage in gold, honey, creamy apricot, tan, and toast for the crescent border of my New Jersey garden, a chance

encounter with *D. parviflora* in Jerry Flintoff's Washington State garden opened my eyes to a whole new world. *D. parviflora* is a Spanish perennial bearing hundreds of tiny bronze flowers, each tipped in gold. The flowers are arranged up and down floral stems, spikes of celadon green flocked in silver. Pre-Internet, it took me a long time to locate a source for these subtle flowers. Through my research, I came across other unusual, perennial foxgloves with flowers in unconventional colors. A perennial species that is offered in catalogs and at the garden center is *D. ferruginea*, called rusty foxglove. This plant's slender spire, 4 to 7 feet tall, is covered with yellow-red-brown flowers.

D. grandiflora (synonym *D. ambigua*), unlike the biennials or short-lived perennials, returns year after year with large, creamy yellow flowers on 2-foot-tall plants. *D. obscura*, a woody shrub that resembles a *Penstemon* more than it does a *Digitalis*, has flowers in shades of glowing burnt orange—burnished red in more sunlight, paler beige in less. I've grown *D. obscura* from seed, and once even got a few plants to bloom. But it has failed to survive for long in my garden. I suspect that this foxglove needs super drainage and winter mulch—a deep cover of snow would probably work, but I can't do much about guaranteeing that in my island garden. *D. obscura* is found in various texts with such common names as dusky maid,

OPPOSITE: Woody perennial *Digitalis obscura*, in front of tender perennial yellow-leaved dracaena, a genus which was recently confirmed as a source of a blood thinner and chemicals that kill ulcer bacterium *Helicobacter pylori*.

LEFT: Demure, short-lived perennial foxglove variety *Digitalis* 'John Innes Tetra'.

sunset foxglove, narrow-leaf foxglove, and willow-leaf foxglove.

Nothing inspires a gardener as much as success, and the biennial *D. lanata* is very satisfying in that regard. The color fits the palette of my crescent border perfectly. The plants have an abundance of inch-long flowers, brown with a bright white lip. Although not perennial, *D. lanata* politely self-sows, replacing one parent with a single new progeny. This plant also has a tendency to hybridize with other foxgloves in the garden. Depending on what plant contributed pollen, successive generations tend to have varied flower colors and more than one flowering stalk, occasionally so many that the plant looks like a candelabra.

I would be happy to welcome most foxgloves to my garden, but a few species might be thuggish in the wrong place. *D. purpurea* "naturalizes" along the woodland edge and could pose a problem, although I haven't heard any complaints. *D. parviflora* (confusingly listed by some texts as hardy in Zones 4–9; others claim it is frost-tender in Zone 6) self-sows in mild climates and is a potentially invasive plant in California, and thus should not be grown there at all. However, the short-lived perennial has never self-sown in my Zone 6 garden. When I want more plants, I carefully pry away one of the offsets that sporadically appear at the base of a parent plant.

Although poisonous to us, like many other plants the digitalis doesn't harm its

---

RIGHT: The tiny yellow flowers of easy and politely self-sowing 3- to 4-foot tall *Digitalis lutea*, behind a topiary boxwood urn (*Buxus sempervirens* 'Elegantissima')—a no-deer-dine combo.

OPPOSITE: Perennial *Digitalis ferruginea* provides unusual tawny color to a mixed planting of perennials and shrubs.

pollinators. The flowers are nearly always accompanied by bumblebees in my garden. When I peer inside the individual flowers, the devices for pollination are obvious: twin anthers at the top of the flowers deposit pollen on the backs of bees that climb inside the blossoms in search of nectar. The bees in turn share pollen from their last encounter.

As evening descends on the garden, bumblebees that have stayed out late may choose to spend the night in one of the "gloves." If I scan over the flowers at dusk, I usually can find at least one flower hosting a sleeping bee.

ABOVE: Silver-green spires and bronze flowers appear on the Spanish foxglove, *Digitalis parviflora*. An alleged perennial, my plants hang around for a while, producing pups that grow to replace mature plants.

LEFT: Jerry Flintoff's Washington State garden is where I first met the Spanish foxglove.

PART TWO

attractions

The lure of the garden has always
been strong. As a child, I eagerly
awaited the colors and scents of spring,
imagining they heralded a spectacle of
blossom and bloom meant just for me.
Summers were spent spying on bees
as they buzzed from flower to flower,
and butterflies as they sipped nectar
from their blossomed perches. Now,
as a passionate gardener and nature's
observer, I know of course it's not for
me these plants are blooming—it's for
the bee, butterfly, ants, birds, bats, and
myriad other creatures that plants need
in order to thrive. And yet, sometimes,
when a particular bloom unfurls, I still
like to imagine it's nature's gift to me, in
return for my time and devotion.

OPPOSITE: Bumblebees can hold on to the disc of purple coneflowers and sleep
through the night.

PARTNERSHIPS

I remember the bumblebees that would visit my rooftop garden when I lived in the SoHo neighborhood of Manhattan in the 1980s. Somehow, these insects—searching for a rare botanical encounter in the urban landscape—managed to find nectar- and pollen-bearing plants flowering in tubs seven stories above the city streets. Little seemed to bother the busy bees, certainly not me, but rain was their enemy. Fur-soaked, they'd drop out of the sky, and on more than one occasion, I would gently scoop one up with a trowel and move it to a sheltered spot to dry off.

On summer evenings, hours before dark, the bees would find places to settle for the night, hugging the spiky center of the purple coneflower, perhaps. If they were resting within reach, I couldn't resist countering better judgment and petting the avian teddy bears as they slept.

Despite the time spent together in that rooftop garden, I knew that the bumblebees weren't pets, and that their delightful behavior had nothing to do with me. The bees that were visiting my garden were following nature's prime directive: to perpetuate the species, and in this case, that meant plants.

Natural plant propagation may seem fairly straightforward: plants grow, bloom, male parts meet female parts often with the help of a bee, seeds develop, fall, sprout, and the cycle begins all over again. But it is not always that simple.

I can't help but be amazed by the elaborate means some plants resort to in order to produce seeds. There are sexual subterfuges, for instance—plants that produce simulated pheromones, chemical sex lures, to attract pollinators. But many other plants do *not* depend on animals at all. The conifers, for example, such as pines, cycads, and cedars, evolved earlier than flowering plants and their pollinators. When ready, these plants release pollen in clouds, relying on the wind to carry it to immature female cones. Although this method may seem to leave too much to chance, it's clearly worked well for the conifers, which are still around today.

Plants need to survive, but for them to thrive as well often means finding better places to grow. The way plants do this is by moving, traveling, with seeds floating on the wind or on water. Other plants produce sweet fruit to attract animals such as birds to transport their seeds to far-off places.

We surmise that these relationships have evolved through happy accidents, like a mutation that makes one species have a slightly better chance of success in its environment. Maybe on one day, one plant that usually has green fruit produces a bright red berry, and perhaps one recently born bird has an ability to see red from a greater distance than its brethren. The bird eats the berry and passes the seeds through its gut, *and* also passes its visual ability down through generations.

The bird-meets-berry example may seem coincidental, but there are greater forces at work here. In this blending of genes and genetic information, nature hopes to select a little improvement from here, and another one from there, so the offspring—a hybrid—has a better chance for adaptation and may very well acquire the best attributes of both parents along the way. We do not know whether the red fruit or the fortunate bird with its special ability came first. It is a chicken-or-egg phenomenon. Good luck, as they say, is taking advantage of opportunity.

ROOM FOR IMPROVEMENT

When I hear the word *hybrid,* I first think of all those allegedly "new and improved" tomatoes and marigolds that graced the covers of seed catalogs when I was a kid. Back then, most gardeners, like farmers, grew their plants from seeds. These folks remembered the Victory Gardens of World War II, when 20 million Americans who had never grown food before dug into the soil in backyards, empty lots, and even city rooftops in the name of patriotism.

After World War II, everything old was out, anything new was in; nurseries promised healthier varieties with larger, juicier fruit, more flowers, more colors, and annuals that made it from seed to vase faster than last year's model. Unfortunately, Americans who were used to starting plants from seed left behind a generation of gardeners frightened of propagation and happy to shell out much more money for faster results from live plants—leaving the "dirty work" to someone else.

In the last 20 years or so, consumers seem to have gotten wise to the fact that "new" is not always "improved." Today's gardeners are less likely to grow a plant just because we're told to, or to be first on the block to display a hot new annual. But true rarity has its fans. We are now just as likely to try to grow something for the challenge—because it might be next to impossible to cultivate, for our own satisfaction, and perhaps for a bit of competition among like-minded members of our particular fancy's club. However, we also know, now, that hoarding a plant usually leads to losing the plant. The best way to save a plant is to give it away, or at least a piece of it, and then you can get some back if you lose it.

ABOVE: Most seedlings are a hybrid genetic blending of distinct individuals.

OPPOSITE, CLOCKWISE FROM TOP LEFT: Berries like those of *Aralia racemosa* attract birds that carry the seeds away to find new, and perhaps better, places to grow.

The seeds of milkweed are attached to fluff that becomes airborne. This soft material was used by early colonists for pillow stuffing.

The most extreme hybrid mixes two genera, and is usually bred with the help of humans—in this case Terra Nova Nursery with contributions from *Heuchera* (color) and *Tiarella* (vigor and form) to make *Heucherella* 'Stoplight'.

Mass sowings of seeds may yield individuals with aberrant and delightful characteristics, such as striped *Canna* 'Pretoria'.

PRECEDING PAGE: An old German postcard features a foxglove and a bee.

There is also a renewed interest in "old" plant varieties among baby boomers looking for antique varieties and heirloom strains instead of the latest touted F1 hybrid. With the shift in gardeners' mindset, messing with nature has gotten a bad name. To many gardeners, a hybrid is something cooked up in a laboratory, like a three-headed sunflower. But the heirloom strains are also hybrids, as is every new organism that is the product of a sexual union. When a male gamete (pollen grain, or spermatozoa) from one entity fertilizes a female gamete (ovum, or egg), a hybrid is produced, which may look exactly like its parents or exhibit noticeably different characteristics.

An *intraspecific* hybrid is the result of having two parents in the same species, like all of us humans. An *interspecific* hybrid comes about when a botanist, or nature occasionally, cross-pollinates two plants from the same genus but not the same species. (The new *Echinacea* hybrid coneflowers bred by Dr. James Ault of the Chicago Botanic Garden are an example.) Hybrids of two different but closely related genera very rarely happen in nature but have been produced by diligent and patient hybridizers. *Fatshedera*, a cross between *Fatsia* and *Hedera*, is an example of these kind of *intergeneric* or *bigeneric* hybrids, as are the *Heucherella* hybrids—crosses between closely related *Heuchera* and *Tiarella*, combining the vivid foliage of the former with the reliability of the latter and producing vigorous, dramatically colorful, floriferous "new" plants.

What does all this mingling mean to today's gardener? Well, if you are a daylily fancier and believe there can never be too much of a good thing, you can select from some 50,000 hybrids made by professional and amateur hybridizers who usually cross varieties that have descended from only a handful of *Hemerocallis* species. Or, if the native Eastern dogwood trees on your property have died from fungal anthracnose, as some of mine have, then you might look to the disease-resistant intraspecific hybrids bred by Dr. Elwin Orton of Rutgers University in New Jersey. Dr. Orton crossed the midspring-blooming North American *Cornus florida*, with the late-spring- to summer-blooming Asian species *C. kousa*, which is not susceptible to the same diseases. These trees are disease resistant, and they also bridge the blooming season of the two species, beginning to flower as the Eastern dogwoods finish and when the Asian trees start to blossom.

In the end, what makes a new plant a permanent member of the garden is its staying power. If the plant is not just a way to get the consumer to continually buy the next fancy thing, but a garden-worthy perennial, annual, tree, or shrub, then it has value that will last far beyond its first appearance on the market.

OPPOSITE: A handful of daylily species, including the roadside *Hemerocallis fulva*, led to thousands of hybrids.

RIGHT, FROM TOP TO BOTTOM: Intergeneric hybrid x *Fatshedera lizei* is made from *Hedera* (ivy) and *Fatsia*. 'Jungle Beauty' is a near-black daylily hybrid. Dr. Elwin Orton bred disease resistance into native dogwood through crosses with Asian *Cornus kousa*, producing trees like 'Stellar Pink'.

BRIGHT YOUNG THING

In 2004, *Echinacea* 'Orange Meadowbrite' appeared on the market, and it was heralded as a breakthrough color for "purple coneflowers." Dr. James Ault had taken the daisylike American prairie perennial and given it a new color. "*Orange* purple coneflower" sounds oxymoronic, but Dr. Ault, the director of plant research at the Chicago Botanic Garden, had produced more unheard-of colors: coral, cerise, flaxen, gold, mango, tangerine, and glowing sunset.

Hybrids between *Echinacea* species do occur in the wild from time to time, but Dr. Ault suspected that he could enhance the results if he played pollinator. For one parent, he chose *E. purpurea,* the popular garden perennial. For the other, he chose *E. paradoxa,* which has yellow petals and is the only *Echinacea* species that does not bloom in tints of purple (that's the paradox, although we do have white cultivated varieties). The goal was to blend the flower colors to produce orange tones.

When the flowers were ready for pollination, Dr. Ault covered each mother flower-to-be in a clear plastic isolation bag with tiny perforations that allowed air to enter but stopped pollen-bearing insects from polluting his mix. He then brought pollen from a male plant and applied it with a small artist's paintbrush to the flowers on the central disk. The plastic bags remained on the plants after pollination to prevent migrating goldfinches from snacking. The first seeds were collected in 1998, and they produced close to 4,000 plants. As expected, the blossoms of that generation were dirty purplish pink. The target colors of hybrids often do not show up until the second generation.

CONTINUED...

OPPOSITE: Coneflower hybrids of *Echinacea purpurea* and *E. paradoxa.* ABOVE: White purple coneflower, *E. purpurea* 'White Swan'.

The eureka moment came three years later, when seeds from the hybrid plants yielded 50 second-generation flowers in extraordinary shades, ranging from pale to deep orange. They also had an unexpected bonus, apparently from a recessive gene—fragrance. Neither parent has a scent, but the hybrids smelled faintly of orange and clove.

Although you might not be as devoted as Dr. Ault, or need another full-time job, you can try your hand at home hybridizing, perhaps with a daylily, which boldly presents its sexual organs right out front for easy access. Hellebores are another easy option since you can take pollen from one plant, either on a paintbrush or by plucking an entire stamen and

anther covered with ripe pollen with tweezers, and carry it to a receptive stigma, which is easy to find since this female organ is held within a flower that has not yet opened. Squeeze the blossom and look inside. The stigma will be revealed at the center of the flower.

I've hybridized a few hellebores, and more daylilies, just for fun. Dr. Ault used a bag to cover the flowers following pollination, so pollen from plants not included in his experiments would not be delivered to the flowers by bees and pollute his crosses. For the daylily, I don't go to such lengths. The daylily is usually pollinated very soon after its anthers split open with ripe pollen. To avoid self-pollination, I remove the stamens (male organs) when the flower first opens before the anthers reveal the pollen inside, a process I call "gelding the lily." Later, I collect pollen from the anther of another daylily in the garden—the father-to-be—with a paintbrush. I bring the fresh pollen to the female part of the first flower and lightly brush a little onto the stigma (the sticky tip of the pistil). In about a month, a fruit will be ready for seed harvest. The results of the cross can be seen in two or three years when the plant bears its first blooms—fast for a perennial.

ABOVE: *Echinacea* 'Orange Meadowbright' (*E.* 'Art's Pride'). OPPOSITE, CLOCKWISE FROM TOP LEFT: One parent, yellow *Echinacea paradoxa. E. purpurea. Helleborus* x *orientalis* hybrids. Hand-pollinating a female hellebore flower.

mix and mingle

Daylilies are popular for amateurs to hybridize because the sexual organs are large and easy to see and deal with. I can tell just by looking that both male parts (anthers) and the female part (pistil) are together on the same open flower. About three-quarters of all flowering plants have hermaphroditic blossoms like the daylilies; these are called "perfect" in botany. Other flowering plants are *monoecious,* with separate male and female flowers on the same plant. And still other flowering plants are *dioecious,* having male and female flowers on separate plants.

Many plants that have both male and female parts in the same flowers have developed sex organs that ripen and become receptive to pollination at different times to avoid self-pollination. Remember the hellebores? The female stigma of a hellebore flower is ready to accept pollen from another flower a week or more before its own male anthers have produced their fertile grains. Even before the flower opens, bees push their way into the swollen buds in search of pollen, which they do not find, but deposit some from the last ripe anthers they visited. In another strategy, the female organs on some flowers are "self-incompatible," and they can actually recognize and reject their own pollen.

In order for squash plants to bear fruit, pollen from these monoecious plants has to be picked up from a male flower and delivered to a female flower, but bees may also pick up pollen from a neighbor's flower and bring it to a female.

The dioecious plants always mix genes, since these plants are never self-fruitful—male flowers grow on male plants, and female flowers, the ones that make seeds, grow on female plants. If you want to have showy fruit on your winter berry holly, *Ilex verticillata,* for instance, you must have a female, as well as at least one male, a stud holly. So if you grow fruitful 'Scarlet O'Hara', you better have a handsome 'Rhett Butler' ready and waiting.

Species with separate male and female flowers on different plants guarantee what nature hopes for: healthy and efficient offspring. There is a tendency for the strongest genes from both parents, often carrying the most successful characteristics of the population—drought tolerance in a dry area, for instance—to be reflected in the progeny; that's how natural selection works. Mixing genes also leads to diversity, increasing the plants' ability to survive and thrive. Botanists refer to this success as *heterosis.* You may have heard it called hybrid vigor.

ABOVE: Daylilies don't have to be orange anymore, as seen in this lavender-pink hybrid.

OPPOSITE, CLOCKWISE FROM TOP LEFT: Daylily flowers, with sexual organs clearly evident, are easy to hybridize. This sienna daylily is 'Lady Lucille'.

Hellebores bear female flower parts while still closed, and then male flowers later.

Ilex verticillata bears bright red berries, but hybridizing with *I. serrata* leads individuals with gold to deep orange berries like 'Aurantiaca' to propagate from cuttings.

From a few Central American squash species, hundreds of colorful hybrids have been bred through millennia.

THE BUZZ

I can hear a bumblebee in the garden before I even see it flying from flower to flower. Although we associate the buzzing noise with bees' rapidly beating wings, the louder sound we hear is actually related to their breathing. Bumblebees have holes on their abdomens called *spiracles*, and it's the air rushing through these openings that creates the most buzz.

Bumblebee flight is an enigma. Their weight-to-wing ratio draws a conclusion—visual evidence to the contrary—that bumblebees simply cannot fly. But even aerodynamic engineers have to admit that they do, and together with their cousins the honeybees, they visit flowers in fields, city gardens, and farms, where their relationship to us humans is essential, since much of what we eat depends on them for pollination. It's estimated that honeybees and bumblebees, through their pollination efforts, contribute between $10 million and $20 billion a year to the U.S. economy. That does not include honey production, which comes primarily from honeybees, since bumblebees make honey for themselves but not enough to share with humans.

Like honeybees, bumblebees are important pollinators. These insects sip nectar from one flower, getting pollen all over themselves in the process, and then fly off to another flower, where they inevitably leave some of the pollen behind on the sticky female stigmas. But bumblebees are also avian allies of some plants through a means of pollination that honeybees cannot perform: *sonication* using vibration, sound to shake pollen free.

Approximately 8 percent of *all* flowers require sonication—resonant vibration—also called buzz pollination. For example, tomato plants grown in greenhouses need help getting their flowers pollinated. Outdoors, wind will make the flowers move, which shakes the pollen free to fall to the stigma below. But under glass, some growers use vibrating benches, while others bring in beneficial insects such as the bumblebee. When vibrating inside a flower, most of the pollen gets knocked down to the pistil and stigma, but some ends up on the hairs of the bee, is collected in baskets on the insect's rear legs, and may also be transported to the next flower and deposited during the subsequent pollination shakedown.

see the light

Bees are attracted to the color blue, from flowers such as Virginia bluebells, lungwort, and other members of the borage family. These plants often have pink buds

LEFT: Some flowers like cranberry (top), tomato (center), and *Geranium phaeum* (bottom) are "buzz pollinated." The hum of the bee, a sound made by abdominal vibrations, shakes pollen loose from anthers to pistil.

OPPOSITE: A bumblebee luxuriates in *Dahlia* pollen—guaranteeing fruit and seeds.

Bees are under attack. The honeybee has been stricken by fatal mite infestations in the recent past. And now we are facing the mysterious "colony collapse syndrome," which is  decimating hives around the United States and Europe. I rarely see these bees in the garden anymore. The bumblebees are victims of insecticide poisonings and loss of habitat. In Great Britain, the rate of bumblebee decline is troubling. Britain and Ireland used to have 25 native species, 3 of which have become extinct during the last 20 years. Nine species are on a watch list, and 15 are noted to have had serious habitat loss. "Bumblebees are fascinating and beautiful insects that deserve conserving in their own right," says Ben Darvill, cofounder and conservation manager of Britain's Bumblebee Conservation Trust. "But there are far more pressing ecological and economic reasons to halt their decline. If bumblebees continue to disappear our native plants will set less seed, potentially resulting in gradual but sweeping changes to the countryside," Darvill warns. "Indeed, there is evidence that this process is already under way."

What can we do? First and foremost, do not use pesticides, and even if organic ones are sprayed, check labels so that spraying does not coincide with times when bees are active. Don't be quick to kill broadleaf weeds in grass lawn. Frankly, if you are not making a putting green, I see no reason for the general use of herbicides in lawn at all. The clovers, which were once considered lawn in themselves, began to be eradicated after World War II, when herbicide manufacturers convinced Americans that lawns should be made of grass plants alone.

To further aid the cause, collect lawn clippings and sprinkle them in small piles beneath shrubs, where they might be adopted as nesting sites for some species. Other bumblebees nest underground, so do not disturb abandoned mouse holes and the like

(unless occupied by wasps in a part of the garden where you need to hang out). Unlike wasps and honeybees, a self-confident, docile bumblebee rarely attacks and has to be quite bothered to sting a person. Also, unlike sacrificial honeybees, which sting and die, bumblebees do not perish if they use their stingers.

Perhaps the best thing to do is plant flowers that these invertebrates like to visit. In early spring, flowering bulbs and shrubs such as pussy willow may attract queens who are in search of a place to start a new colony. Members of the rose family, apples, pears, coto-neaster, and roses themselves are favorites, but be sure to include single-flowered rose species and varieties, as these afford easier access to pollen. Herbs are also among the more popular plants, with members of the borage and mint families topping the list.

OPPOSITE: Bumblebees filling honey bee gap. ABOVE LEFT: Strawberry flower pollination depends on bees. ABOVE RIGHT: Natural honey bee hive in tree hollow.

One way to tell a moth from a butterfly, regardless of color or comeliness, is to observe it at rest: A butterfly brings its wings up to a vertical position when it settles; a moth rests its wings flat.

Plants that attract butterflies use sweet fragrance and bright color rather than an abundance of pollen. The flowers of these butterfly lures are shaped like little cups, or they may have long spurs, like the columbine's, that require the butterfly to unroll its coiled tongue. Most butterfly-pollinated flowers also provide a place for the animals to alight—plants with outer petals such as the daisy, for instance, and flowers like those of dill and fennel that bloom in umbels, umbrella-shaped clusters of flowers typified by members of the carrot family. Butterflies see not only the colors we do, but also ultraviolet and polarized light. The former shows patterns indicating the location of the nectaries in the flower. The polarizing capabilities filter out some reflected light so that the insects see angles of colored light from greater distances to help them find the sweet food that sustains them.

ACUTE SYMBIOSIS

Nearly one out of every ten flowering plant species is in the orchid family (Orchidaceae). Although they were once thought to be relative newcomers in the plant world, recent DNA analysis shows that Orchidaceae members were around with the dinosaurs, and may actually be among the earliest flowering plants on Earth. Like nearly all success stories in botany, it comes down to sex and partnerships. Orchids have evolved very explicit reproductive strategies—first for pollination, and then for germination—that have helped them persist for 40 million years.

Indoors I grow a hybrid tropical *Oncidium* orchid with long, wiry, branched stems covered with airy yellow blossoms that dance in the slightest breeze. When these flowers wiggle in the wild, bees perceive them as interlopers invading their territory and they attack. During the skirmish, the blossoms are pollinated.

Some *Paphiopedilum* slipper orchids, including those grown as houseplants, have little spots on their petals that could be mistaken for aphids. These attract species of ants that herd aphids and "milk" them for their sweet secretion, called honeydew. Wasps likewise prey on and eat aphids, as do ladybugs. Some species of flies lay their eggs on aphids. Any of these insects may slip and fall into the pouch of the "paph's" flower, lined with downward-facing hairs that make a short stay inside unavoidable. In order to escape, the trapped insect must climb through a slender passageway where it picks up and delivers pollen, an ingenious example of nature's design.

RIGHT: Although all cacti originated in the Americas, not all cacti live in the desert, or even in dry places. Some like *Epiphyllum* come from jungles where they are bat pollinated.

A MATTER OF TASTE

When choosing plants to attract butterflies, select vividly colorful flowers that are rich in nectar and offer a comfortable place to land. The all-time plant champion is the butterfly bush, *Buddleia* species. These shrubs of varying hardiness have deep, rich scents of baby powder, cherries, and a hint of wood—similar to the intensely fragrant heliotropes.

But the *Buddleia* species and varieties can self-seed freely and may become invasive, which has led a few regions of the country to ban their planting. Hybridizers at Cornell University are attempting to develop new varieties that will not produce viable seed.

There are plenty of other noninvasive butterfly magnets, and some are likely to be native to your region, including Joe Pye weed, monarda (bee balm), and purple coneflower. Plants in the genus *Asclepias* are members of the milkweed family (Asclepiadaceae). The butterfly weed (*Asclepias tuberosa*) attracts with its bright orange color. This U.S. native once grew wild in all but seven northern and midwestern states; it is now gone from Maine, endangered in New Hampshire, and threatened in Vermont. The swamp milkweed (*A. incarnata*) grows 3 to 4 feet tall, bears either reddish mauve or white flowers, is an excellent plant for moist spots in sun, and is frequently available from mail-order sources and at nurseries.

Another thing to consider if you wish to have butterflies in your garden is the crawlers that precede them—caterpillars. Many of the milkweeds have not only flowers that feed adults but leaves for the larvae to snack on as well. The common milkweed, *A. syriaca*, is the preferred host to the monarch butterfly caterpillar. The plant is toxic, but not to the caterpillars that eat the leaves and incorporate the toxins, which makes the caterpillars bad tasting and even poisonous to potential prey. Birds quickly learn to avoid the larvae, which advertise their danger with memorable, contrasting stripes of chartreuse and black.

To ensure a steady stream of butterflies in the garden, include a plant or two to feed the larvae. Think of these larvae as an excellent opportunity to teach children that all stages of an animal's life are important. Perhaps it is best to start with the prettiest part of the life cycle, the flying fritillaries—butterflies. In the summer, when butterflies visit, you can place a few slices of very ripe banana in a shallow dish set in an open, elevated spot. Butterflies will flock to the fragrant fruit, much to the delight of kids.

OPPOSITE, CLOCKWISE FROM TOP: Butterfly-attracting Joe Pye weed, *Eupatorium* 'Gateway'. Monarch larva derives toxicity from milkweed host. Butterfly sipping nectar.

The flowers of other orchids have evolved to mimic the female of insect species, incorporating her color, scent, shape, and feel in order to lure male insects that will attempt to copulate. These orchids produce little sacs of pollen, called *pollinia*, that become glued to the backs of the males as they leave to fly to another alluring and receptive orchid, where a special hook on that plant's flower plucks off the pollinia.

When all goes according to plan, orchids produce dry fruits filled with microscopic seeds. Most plants produce seeds that include a ready supply of nutrients, like the yolk of an egg or the starch in a bean. The nutrients nourish the sprouting seed as it sends down a developing radicle, a young root that will eventually absorb food from the soil. Orchid seeds do not have built-in stores and do not even produce a radicle, so they must be fed by other means.

In nature, orchid seeds receive their necessary life support from symbiotic fungi. You may have even seen some of these fungi—white threads in the mulch or in small clumps of soil—when moving a woodland wildflower without realizing the great part they play in the lives of all plants. Obviously, plants cannot eat the leaves that fall to the ground. The debris must be broken down and rendered into elements that plant roots can absorb, and that is what the fungi do.

While it's nearly impossible to re-create nature's symbiotic relationship with the orchid, it is possible to provide the necessary nutrients by other means. Professional growers sow seed in a specialized, enriched Jell-O–like agar medium placed in a sterilized flask. Tropical greenhouse and houseplant orchids have been propagated using this method for decades, and a few nurseries are now growing our native, hardy terrestrial orchids this way. I never bought a hardy native terrestrial orchid until nursery-propagated plants came on the market in the late 1990s. Before this time, orchids offered for sale were wild-collected, which not only was unethical, and in some places illegal, but it was also often a death sentence for the plants, some of which are just about impossible to transplant.

Today I grow a few North American *Cypripedium* orchids, among them *C. kentuckiense*, which has a very large saclike lower appendage, as big as a jumbo hen's egg. Most of the species do well in the acidic organic soil in my woodland garden. The showy lady's slipper (*C. reginae*) is an exception. This spectacular plant grows happily next to the limestone wall on the outside of the gravel garden—producing more flowers every year. Unlike the other woodland species, this one is not an acid lover but likes neutral to alkaline soil. Bill Cullina, the head propagator for The Garden in the Woods, the Massachusetts headquarters of the New England Wild Flower Society, grows dozens of these plants in his vegetable garden.

LEFT: *Oncidium* flowers mimic flying insects when they flutter, inviting attack from pollinators (top); *Paphiopedilum* have aphid-like dots that attract predators (center and bottom).

OPPOSITE, CLOCKWISE FROM LEFT: *Cypripedium kentuckiense* grows easy in woodland soil. *C. reginae* is a good garden plant for moist alkaline soil. A cluster of *C. kentuckiense*.

WELCOME GUESTS

Although I am not a big fan of plants that self-sow, dropping their seeds on the ground, where they sprout—whether I want them there or not—I know many gardeners who delight in the surprises they find year after year in their flower gardens. But some plants may oversow and become invasive weeds; I've been pulling out *Nigela damascena*, love-in-a-mist, for five years now. Self-sown volunteers can always be shared with fellow gardeners, a practice that gave rise to the term "Pass-Along Plants." But to my mind, the phrase could be recast as "Pass-Along Pests," because the plants we have too many of are frequently the ones we are most anxious to share. And these could go on to make nuisances of themselves in an unsuspecting friend's garden.

All that said, I consider short-lived perennial and monocarpic plants (annuals and biennials that grow, flower, set seed, and die) that seem to replace this year's individual with a single entity the following spring to be well behaved and acceptable. My semi-perennial columbines do that, as does my white-flowered strain of rose campion and a few biennial verbascums and foxgloves.

But other hardy (cold-tolerant) annuals and biennials that I wish replaced themselves do not. The biennial *Salvia sclarea*, clary sage, fails to return from fallen seeds. Even the annual opium poppies do not return without my help.

When these plants have finished blooming and are just beginning to turn brown, I place inverted paper bags over them and tie the bags shut around the stems. I cut the stems in a week or so and bring them indoors, where I turn the bags right-side-up and hang them in a well-ventilated place. The seed heads continue to dry and the bags catch any falling seeds.

After a few months, I open the bags, shake the stems of the seedpods until they stop pouring out seeds, and remove them from the bag. Then I let the seed collect in one corner of the bag and carefully pour the contents into an envelope labeled with the date and the

ABOVE: Candelabra-form hybrid *Verbascum*. OPPOSITE, LEFT TO RIGHT: Biennials Miss Wilmott's Ghost (*Eryngium giganteum*), clary sage (*Salvia sclarea*), and silver mullein (*Verbascum bombyciferum*).

name of the plant. The envelopes are sealed, folded, and placed into a glass jar. Then they go into the refrigerator until March.

I harvest and store *Eryngium giganteum* seeds when the flower heads are dry and sow them at the end of winter, indoors or in situ. I repeat this process every year to guarantee that I will have blooming biennial *Eryngium* by summer. This is an undertaking well worth the effort, as the plant, with its silvery leaves and spiny bracts etched in platinum over celadon green, is especially beautiful. The bracts are surrounded by a 2-inch-tall cone that bears scores of tiny white flowers over a period of several weeks. As the plant branches, it produces a dozen or so smaller collars and cones around the first large one. Despite its appearance, the common name for this the genus is "sea holly," but the favorite moniker for this species is not as descriptive as "thimble holly" or "silver ruff" but "Miss Willmott's Ghost," after a well-known British gardener and designer of the late 19th and early 20th century.

Ellen Willmott reputedly collected and then surreptitiously scattered seeds of her favorite sea holly while visiting other people's gardens. Later, the ghostly silver plants mysteriously appeared. If you grow this striking plant, and it does return for you, then your climate must be right for it (or your garden's been visited by the ghostly Miss Willmott).

My garden is visited by what seems to be every nectar-seeking, pollinating flying insect in the state of New Jersey when Miss Willmott's perennial cousin *E. planum* 'Blaukappa' begins to bloom. The tiny blue flowers of 'Blaukappa' cover an iridescent ball the size of a marble, nestled on a spiny, steel blue bract at the end of every stem. Saving seeds from this plant might produce interesting results, but you will not get an offspring that is identical to its parent. Taking root cuttings from the plant (see page 137) will produce offspring identical to the parent and ensure repeat performances from the plant and its aerial pollinators.

ABOVE: Many conifers are evergreen, but others like the swamp cypress (*Taxodium distichum*) are deciduous, with showy autumn colors. These plants are gymnosperms, having naked seed in their cones. Conifers have airborne pollen, and rely on their numbers to help males and females connect. Millions of pollen grains are produced, as allergy sufferers know well.

LEFT: The swamp cypress does not need to be grown in water and is tolerant of poorly or well-drained soil. In my garden, it grows in sandy soil.

BROADCAST MUSE

Plants expend a lot of energy producing viable reproductive material and advertising this through their flowers—elaborate vessels designed to lure pollinators; just consider a huge flaring lily. But some plants put their effort into quantity over quality, adopting a shotgun approach to propagation. Pines, spruces, firs, and other needle evergreens, for example, generate massive amounts of pollen grains to flood the air, so much the better to connect with a female of the same species.

Conifers are gymnosperms; they do not produce flowers or fruits but rather "naked seed." We know them as cone-bearing trees, often with evergreen needles, like pines and hemlocks. But some are deciduous, like the beautiful larch (*Larix* species) and the underappreciated, versatile, and handsome swamp cypress (*Taxodium* species); the latter naturally occurs in moist places but makes a good suburban street tree as well.

Grass-family plants such as rice, wheat, and corn are angiosperms; they produce flowers and fruits. The flowers are often insignificant, and so grass plants, like the conifers that evolved eons before them, depend on the wind for pollination.

Grasses and conifers have a symbiotic (if somewhat capricious) relationship with the wind. I suppose that in the environments where the grasses evolved, such as the savannas of the Serengeti Plains in Tanzania or the tall- and short-grass prairies of Wisconsin or Nebraska, flying insect pollinators were less common (or less successful in the ever present, often overpowering winds), and therefore grasses did not adapt to depend on them and had no reason to put their energy into showy or fragrant blossoms. Instead, grasses put their muscle into creating vast quantities of genetic material, pollen, and to growing in large colonies to improve their chances of connecting sperm to egg.

Many broad-leaved deciduous trees, among them the maple, birch, and oaks, are also wind pollinated. These trees produce so much pollen that there is enough to cover our cars with yellow dust and aggravate people with allergies. Late summer's ragweed (*Ambrosia*, a lovely name) is another allergy inducer that is wind pollinated. Some people believe that goldenrod is the menace, but that plant is only guilty by association; it blooms in similar places as ragweed, has a somewhat similar growth habit, and blooms at the same time. But the large pollen grains of goldenrod do not become airborne; these members of the Asteraceae or daisy family require insects to carry the pollen from plant to plant. When you see advertisements for allergy medicines showing people enjoying the scent of double roses again after taking a magic pill to cure their hay fever, it is another Madison Avenue fabrication. The pretty flowers do not rely on the wind to scatter their pollen; they have evolved their colorful blossoms to attract pollinators who happily provide matchmaking services.

IT TAKES GALL

Before the printing press was invented, Christian monks painstakingly reproduced documents by hand. Such practices were associated with spiritual ritual, and the making of ink was filled with the symbolism of transformation, as raw ingredients melded with the physical, mental, and spiritual state of the maker. In Christian symbolism, the bee was thought to die at the end of summer and, like Jesus, be resurrected in spring. Pollination was likened to the spreading of God's word. The bee's industry was associated with goodness, the virgin female workers with Mary, and the hive with the Church. On the other hand, the wasp was a good-for-nothing scavenger. The mighty oak, it was thought, produced the gall around the evil wasp's egg to protect itself from certain destruction, thus thwarting the spread of evil. Medieval scribes transformed the oak gall into ink, creating a purpose for the insect.

The recipe for oak gall ink included 12 parts rainwater, 3 parts by volume ground oak galls, 2 parts ferrous sulfate, 1 part powdered gum arabic (an emulsifier made from acacia tree species), and eggshells. The water was brought to a boil and the ground oak gall added. After 15 minutes, the ferrous sulfate was added. The liquid was next poured through a cloth filter; a little bit of it was added to the gum arabic until it thoroughly dissolved, and then that was added to the rest of the liquid. The concoction was poured into a bottle, sealed, stored, and aged. If the ink was too acidic it would destroy the material it was being applied to, so eggshells, which are alkaline, were added to the ink.

After about six months, the ink was strained and ready for use, but it wasn't purely black at that time; it was sepia brown and continued to darken over time, both in the bottle and on the paper or parchment. Sediments in the bottom of the jar had to be stirred to keep them in suspension, but urine was often added to homogenize the ink. The best galls for color were collected early in the season while the wasp larvae were still inside.

With the making of ink, recording and disseminating the words of God, the wasps were no longer creatures of evil. The insects became evangelical collaborators—instruments for good—helping to spread the gospel.

STRANGER THAN FICTION

My friends Jean and Dan Pope live on a hilltop in Pennsylvania at a bend in the Susquehanna River. The couple has a large edible-fig tree that they summer on their porch and winter inside next to windows facing their spectacular view. When I visited them, I asked about fruit production. Dan said they have fruit every year, but he'd never seen the plant's flowers. I told him, "You're eating them."

Fig fruits are actually composed of an outer skin (a modified stem) encasing hundreds of minute flowers—a kind of "inside-out" inflorescence. Most figs require assistance from a tiny wasp in order to be pollinated. Opposite the stem end of the bulbous flower/vessel, called a *syconium*, is a little hole called the *ostiole* through which a fig wasp climbs to lay her eggs, pollinating the flowers in the process. Once pollinated, the minuscule flowers produce hundreds of seeds. Cutting a fig in half, you'll see a hollow area with seeds where the flowers once grew.

Speculation abounds on what happens after pollination: the mother wasp escapes back out through the hole; or she spends the winter hibernating in the fruit; or, as is often proposed, she and the developing larvae are digested by enzymes inside the fruit and are therefore never evident to us. But if that were the case, there wouldn't be any fig wasps. The true tale is more bizarre.

The tiny female wasp, small enough to fly through the eye of a needle, pushes her way through the ostiole, losing her wings and antennae in the bargain. Inside, there are three types of flowers: short female flowers, tall female flowers, and male flowers clustered around the entrance to the syconium. The wasp inserts her ovipositor into the styles of the female flowers, but it is too short to reach the bottom of the tall female flowers, and she moves to the next, shorter flower, where she deposits an egg and hormones inducing the flower to develop a gall (see page 112) around the developing baby wasp. In the process, the mother wasp leaves a bit of pollen from her birthplace on the tall flowers, which go on to develop seeds. Then, after all that work in a very short time, she dies.

When male wasps hatch, they chew their way out of their galls and search for galls containing females. They make a small hole in each gall and fertilize the females, and then they either enlarge the holes to release the females or in some species leave the fertilized females to chew their own way out. The newly hatched females immediately find pollen with their antennae and collect it into sacs on the undersides of their bodies. Meanwhile, the males gnaw a larger hole in the ostiole, climb out, and die. The females fly away, in search of a new fig syconium, and the process begins again. The entire life of the adult female wasp may last only a few hours.

TOP TO BOTTOM: Fig leaves have been seen in art for centuries and then as Victorian art-cover-ups. The fig fruit is a kind of an inside-out flower—with its sex organs on the interior. My favorite decorative variety is the clown fig (*Ficus aspera* 'Parcellii'), a houseplant shrub with variegated leaves and fruit for warm, humid, and sunny places.

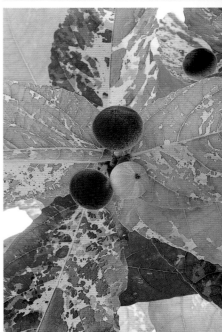

Another version of the pollination story is also true: most edible figs are self-fruitful, self-pollinating, no wasp need apply. The crunchy bits we enjoy when we eat a fig are seeds, not the bodies of deceased arthropods.

'Brown Turkey' is the dwarf edible fig that I grow; it is a compact plant and about the best variety to try in a container. If the season is long enough, it will bear more than one crop of small, sweet brown fruits. Mine lives in a terra-cotta pot, which I move into the dark, unheated basement (roughly 50 degrees F) each fall after the plant drops its leaves outside. A little too early for its own good, the leaf buds and "flower buds" of my plant swell in the dark basement around March, but frosts can occur until mid-May, so I must keep it protected indoors. I usually take it outside to a sheltered place in April, because the plant needs every possible hour of daylight in our short growing season to produce fruit. More than once I have lost every early-developing fruit to a touch of frost, but thankfully, the plant produces another round, and I'm able to pick a handful of figs days before the frosts return in autumn.

LONESTARS AND HITCHHIKERS

Just as plants conscript animals such as wasps, bees, and birds and forces of nature like wind and water for pollination, many seek out similar aid for dispersing seeds and germination.

Hardy cyclamen are geophytes, which means they grow from an underground storage facility, in this case called a tuber, like a potato. I grow some tubers of *Cyclamen hederifolium* (ivy-leaved cyclamen) at the base of the ash tree in the woodland bed. My plants were purchased from American growers who propagated them from seeds. For more than one hundred years, cyclamen tubers were scraped off hillsides and mountains in remote areas of Turkey, and some still are. By 1986, an estimated 70 million wild bulbs and tubers had been sold. International pressure from conservation groups and consumers demanding nursery-propagated tubers rather than wild-collected specimens has been the impetus for Turkish farmers to grow cyclamen from seed, which is actually easier than collecting them.

The flowers that bloom in late summer resemble those of florists' cyclamen, only miniaturized. As the pink or white flowers are blooming, the leaves emerge. If a mild winter follows, the elegant leaves of malachite green with silver or pewter gray veins and mottling (no two plants' leaves are the same) will look good through spring, when the plants become dormant.

When a hardy cyclamen bloom is pollinated, the flower stem spirals and coils up tightly, holding the developing fruits and seeds close to the protective center of the plant. When the fruit is ripe and seeds are ready, the coil relaxes and extends its long stem to lay the fruit on the ground—lying in wait for its specific insect partner. Cyclamen seeds require darkness for germination, and ants are more than happy to oblige. Attracted by the elaiosome, a sugary protein and fat-rich outer ridge on the seed, the

ants collect and carry the seeds to their underground burrows. There they eat away only the sweet part, feeding it to their larvae, and discard the unharmed seeds in their refuse tunnel, which just happens to have the perfect compost and darkness for a germinating cyclamen seed. North American trillium use a similar strategy.

Larger animals such as birds and mammals pick and eat fruits and carry seeds in their digestive tracts until they are dropped long or short distances from their parent plants. Animals also transport seeds unknowingly. Bidens or tickseed has twin-pronged seed coats that hook on to fur or the trouser cuffs of unsuspecting passersby. And who has not wrestled with getting a cocklebur off a canine? This burr, hoarding its seeds inside, has hundreds of hooks that relentlessly attach to longhair coats, and was actually the inspiration for Velcro.

There are also the independent types, plants that go it alone. A few plants simply drop their seeds to the ground around the current generation—a location that has already proved to be welcoming. The peanut and the water arum, for instance, bend their flower stems down to the ground or the water and push the developing fruits into the soil or muck, virtually sowing themselves. Violets, on the other hand, leave nothing to chance. They've evolved to bear two kinds of fruits. The early fruits face upward and explode when ripe, bursting their seams in a violent action that sends seeds up to 6 feet off into uncharted territory in hopes of finding new, hospitable ground. The second fruits grow at the base of the plant and face downward. Like college kids who return home after graduation, these ripe fruits hedge their bets by simply dropping their seeds in a location already tested and proved to be suitable by their parent.

As any lawn lover knows, dandelion parachutes strike out on their own, rising above the grass to catch the wind and cause problems elsewhere. The milkweed's seed, attached to its downy fluff, also takes to the air, even though it is many times the weight of the dandelion's. Aquatic plants often have seeds that float and are carried away by the current until they catch on a bit of debris, sprout, and take root. The largest seed of any plant, the coconut, can float for thousands of miles, surviving in salt water on its own internal reservoir of fresh water.

TOLERANCE

Plenty of animals gather seeds to store over winter, and many of these seeds get forgotten or misplaced. I've heard that squirrels simply forget where they've buried some of their acorns, but I've also read that they intentionally hide extras in case there is a particularly long or harsh winter. The animals may actually bury tasty, less acidic seeds to dig up first and store the harsher, tannin-loaded acorns for emergencies.

Smart or not, cute or not, squirrels drive me nuts, especially when they dig into pots and soil behind the house in Brooklyn, and toss the plants over their shoulders in order to install fruits of the willow oaks from two streets away. Or how about the window frame they gnawed through trying to get inside to the warmth of the office all winter, and inside to the air-conditioned office all summer? You can't live with them, and you can't shoot them, at least not in Brooklyn.

I have found that scented fabric-softening sheets hung on small metal stakes do a very good job of preventing the squirrels from digging in the New Jersey woodland garden. Of course, the beds do not look very nice covered by white flags. And although the fragrance has done a good job of keeping the squirrels at bay, it keeps me away as well.

I must be grateful to the squirrels for something, I suppose. As the planet warms, squirrels will no doubt migrate north and slowly move their acorn stores northward as well, thus extending the oak's range. As older northern oak trees die in areas that become too warm for them, new ones in colder places may survive. But that kind of tree migration takes time, time the oak trees may not have.

mighty oak

Oak trees, whether living or dead, provide shelter to countless creatures, but the tree's greatest contribution is its dry fruit, the acorn. Just like the oak's leaves, all the acorns look different, some with furry cups, others with long, slender nuts. In

RIGHT: Oak leaves and acorns are different depending on the species. Some fruit are tiny, others large and covered by the cap. The leaves vary from rounded to deeply lobed. The blue-green leaf and acorn shown have been plated in copper.

OPPOSITE: The oak is the symbol of strength and long life, but sometimes their endurance is tested. "Live oaks" of the southern and western United States are evergreen trees, or semi-evergreen, dropping old leaves as new ones emerge in spring. These trees in Louisiana, like most oaks, can live a very long time, barring disaster.

its effort to produce at least one healthy descendant, a mature oak will produce thousands of acorns each year. That means several million acorns never germinate.

Blue jays steal unripe acorns. Insects drill little holes to get at the tender meat. The protein-rich acorns nourish deer, squirrels, and other animals. Nuts containing the most tannin, an acidic compound also used in the tanning of leather, are the least palatable, but American Indians boiled them for hours before making them into mush, meal, or flour. And, of course, the wood is used for lumber and fuel.

A few thousand-year-old specimens of the English oak, *Quercus robur*, survive today in Britain, but entire forests were cut down to build houses, churches, factories, and, most of all, the ships of the English navy. In Elizabethan times, a law was passed to protect oak trees from being cut for fuel, and the practice of coppicing was encouraged as a way of making the oak a renewable energy resource (see "Tough Love" on page 228). Selected young trees were cut down to a stump to produce young shoots called whips. These were harvested for firewood, and the stumps went on to produce new growth that could be harvested again and again.

Q. suber, a frost-tender tree from the western part of the Mediterranean basin, is a renewable resource unique in the plant kingdom. This oak is the source of cork used to make wine bottle stoppers, flooring, the soles of shoes, and more. The bark can be sliced off the trees every 9 to 11 years and, remarkably, grows back.

The oak is tied to human history. The Celts associated wisdom with the oak, and the word *Druid* comes from their word for oak, *dru*. The USS *Constitution* was built from some 2,000 southern live oak trees. The vessel's ability to withstand cannon fire inspired its nickname, "Old Ironsides." But few people today realize that the oak tree figured in the drafting of the Declaration of Independence and the U.S. Constitution—or rather, oak trees with a little help from a fascinating insect, the gall wasp.

At one time, most black ink was made from ground oak tree galls, growths caused by various species of wasps that lay eggs in the new oak leaves and branches while they are expanding in spring. These "gall wasps" inject chemicals that combine with the trees' growth-regulating hormones and cause the cells to form into spherical, fuzzy, or lumpy enlarged growths around the eggs, as round and as small as a pea or as large as an apple, depending on the wasp and oak species. The eggs hatch, and the developing wasp larvae feed on the tissue inside the gall. Besides a bit of cosmetic disfigurement, little damage is done to the tree. This is a case of a symbiotic relationship between an insect and a plant, but one that may have benefited people most of all.

LEFT: This majestic southern live oak (*Quercus virginiana*) dripping with tiny bromeliads—Spanish moss (*Tillandsia usneoides*)—holds a swinging bench from one of its lower branches. Trees like these are America's treasures, our pyramids.

SCENTSATIONAL

Entering the garden can be a stirring experience, as all of my senses are ignited by what I see, hear, and touch. Colorful leaves burnished bronze by the late-afternoon sunlight take my breath away. The melody in the sound of the wind rustling the tree leaves refreshes my spirit. The river music lulls me to sleep. The silky leaves of the lamb's ears tickle my fingers. These connections are part of the sensuality of the garden. But of all the delights that stimulate the senses, the most alluring and even mysterious to me is scent.

When I meet a flower for the first time, I instinctively lean over to take a sniff. Like many gardeners, I consider fragrance high on my list of plant attributes. When I sample a smell, I automatically analyze it: I might detect a hint of clove, a whiff of burnt sugar, or the sharp scent of turpines, the pine scents.

The ability to recall the scent of a familiar plant before it blooms or one just sampled on a walk through the garden is not just a fanciful thought but a physiological fact: the region of the brain that receives signals from scent receptors touches the area associated with memory. Scent is the sense of rememberance, able to summon the past as easily as a faded photograph.

Although scent attracts many a gardener to a particular plant or species, it is not humans, of course, that the plants hope to lure with their enticing aromas. Lovely smells captivate certain pollinators, enticing them to visit, while unpleasant odors invite others. Nature has ingeniously tailored the scent to the pollinator. This means that humans are simply the vicarious recipients of these fragrant pleasures and lucky enough to share them in the garden.

STIMULATING MEMORIES

When planting a bed or border, conventional wisdom says that tall plants should be placed at the back, short plants up front. Yet in one area of my garden where the path narrows, I've planted 5- to 7-foot-tall lilies in the foreground—close to the nose. The varieties I've

brains that continue to be replaced throughout our lives.) I was once able to deliver the lilacs in person, and as she unwrapped the flowers I heard her sigh. She said the scent took her back to her own mother's garden. She took a second whiff, brought her hand up to her chest, and described the fragrance of the flowers perfectly.

"Heaven," she said.

words fail us . . .

"Heaven" is one way to describe a fragrance, but it says more about the smeller than what is being smelled. How can one explain the fragrance of a mock orange (*Philadelphus*), for example, to someone who has never met the flower, or to someone who is "hard-of-smelling"? I wish there were more words to describe scents, which are often the most delightful aspects of favorite plants. Perhaps there are just too many delicately nuanced fragrances to pin down, but I'm convinced there are other challenges at work.

According to some scientific references, every person smells things the same, just like normal, healthy eyes by all accounts see colors alike. However, in my observations, everyone's sense of smell is not quite the same, and people definitely have varying degrees of sensitivity to odor. I have an acute sense of smell, mostly a blessing, a curse at times. My sister, on the other hand, could sleep through bacon frying.

In trying to describe the mock orange, I can easily mention the shrub's height and width, and twiggy growth. One word, "white," tells the flower's color. But when it comes to describing the scent, there are only similes, comparisons to other aromas. The flowers of *Philadelphus coronarius* smell like jasmine, *P. virginalis* smells like honeysuckle, and the native species shrub that seeded itself up by the road, *P. inodorus*, as the name implies, has no scent at all.

ABOVE LEFT TO RIGHT:
Among the most fragrant and bluest common lilac is *Syringa vulgaris* 'President Lincoln'—and the tallest, like its namesake.

Mock orange flowers may smell like honeysuckle; nothing (like U.S. native *Philadelphus inodora*); or jasmine, like the large flowered *P. coronaria* 'Belle Etoile'.

Things may not smell the same to everyone; despite my olfactory sensitivity, I cannot smell the autumn scent of katsura (*Cercidiphyllum*—weeping form 'Magnificum', shown), described by my companions as "caramel."

THE NAME GAME

When small groups of people come to visit my garden, and one flower or another presents the opportunity, I like to ask my guests to describe the scent. The result may be a consensus, although the request more often leads to some lively conversation. My guests might take on a bearded iris, for instance. One person says outright, "Grape soda." Another sniffer emphatically claims that the fragrance is like the old Pepsodent toothpaste. Try the challenge in your garden.

There is a technique used by professional "noses" that will increase sensitivity and prolong the experience of sampling and analyzing fragrances. When you meet a flower, take quick sniffs, rather than a slow inhalation. Sniffing increases our responsiveness to sensory stimuli by up to 1,000 percent. Our scent receptors become anesthetized to a fragrance after just a few moments, and we lose the ability to register the quality and quantity of the smell. (This is one reason why some people put on too much perfume.)

In general, we can fully sample only about three flowers before taking a break. Coffee beans may be used as "palate cleansers," or olfactory bulb restorers. Smelling the beans resets the sense of smell to a new baseline. The smell of your own skin can also work to cleanse the nose, so to speak, between samples in the field.

A favorite plant contestant for the fragrance challenge is *Calycanthus floridus*, a large green shrub also known as Carolina allspice or common sweetshrub. Six feet tall and wide, the shrub has lustrous embossed leaves and inch-wide maroon flowers with pointed petals lining every branch from late spring to early summer, with sporadic blooms appearing through the end of August. The flowers have an intriguing aroma that always elicits responses that invariably differ. I've heard it described as the odor of bubble gum, melon, crushed strawberries, or lacquer thinner, and I can imagine that all those scents are in there. Everyone stands by his or her description with certainty, and so do I. The aroma consistently reminds me of the inside of an oak whiskey barrel like the half-barrel planters sold at the garden center. For me at least, my nose knows best.

ABOVE: Subjectively fragrant *Calycanthus floridus*.

OPPOSITE: The ethereal honeysuckle-scented *Philadelphus virginalis* 'Virginal' has double 1-inch flowers that each last for two weeks or longer.

ABOVE, LEFT TO RIGHT: Native *Rhododendron prinophyllum* flowers have a spicy aroma.

Linnaeus described the smell of onion relatives with the made-up word "Alliaceous" (drumstick allium, *A. sphaerocephalum*).

Many essential oils distilled from flowers and plants are now used for making fine soaps.

Linnaeus tried his hand at naming smells, coining the term "Alliaceous" to describe the sharp, sulfuric acid, tear-inducing odor of onions (which are part of the genus *Allium*). You could try following his example, naming the putrid smell of rotting meat (associated with skunk cabbage and other aroids) "Pute"; or the pungent green scent of chrysanthemum foliage might be described as "Mummy." I'm partial to "Lilicious" to describe the delicious scent of the *Lilium* species.

Gardeners, of course, aren't the only ones who struggle to describe scent. Advertising copy in perfume ads goes to metaphoric heights to describe the way one should feel when he or she wears the fragrance. A gentleman's cologne might have "the careful, muscular cool of a panther." Or a woman's perfume could be "transcendent, immortal—plush velvet and black pearls."

Molecular biologist Luca Turin has written a masterpiece of a handbook called *Parfum: le guide*, a literal analysis of the world's great perfumes. In his description of Chanel No. 5, he writes ". . . a radiant chorus of ylang and rose floating like gold leaf on the chalk-white background . . . a Scythian jewel . . . The drydown fades the way white flowers do, slowly becoming soft and flesh-coloured [sic] . . . It is good, at regular intervals, to refresh one's memory of what unalloyed luxury is about."

I think these scent-poems are delightful, but it is style over substance. It would be more helpful to list evocative similes: the forest floor, the ocean, metal, ammonia, or Grandma.

PERFUMERY

There are ways to capture and preserve the things we love in the garden, with a camera, for instance, or by pressing flowers in a phone book. People who grow

Many of the species grown for perfume production can be planted in our garden beds or in pots to summer outdoors. Among these are plants collectively called *geophytes*, which grow from underground modified stems that store moisture, sugars, and starch. We know them as bulbs, corms, and tubers. Hyacinths, freesias, and narcissus are all geophytes used in perfume, as is the tender tuberose. The species *Polianthes tuberosa,* which bears single flowers, is the most fragrant; the highly aromatic double selection *P. tuberosa* 'The Pearl' is sold for planting in warm-climate gardens (Zones 8 to 10), for forcing as potted plants in colder zones, and for cut-flower production. As cut flowers, the blossoms last a long time, and cutting your own will not hurt the plant; removing the blooms redirects its energy to replenishing the tuber.

The plants bloom in late summer, 90 to 120 days after potting or planting. In cold climates, the bulbs must be dug up from the summer garden, or potted tubers can be taken indoors to a frost-free but cool (around 50 degrees F), dry place (mine are in the basement). I let the tubers overwinter in their pots of dry potting mix.

Hyacinths (*Hyacinthus orientalis*) and daffodils (*Narcissus* species and varieties) are easy to grow in the garden, and they can also be forced into bloom indoors following a period of chilling. To my nose, among the sweetest of the daffodils is the pretty species *N. jonquilla* and its cultivars, such as 'Sailboat'. Jonquils are delicate and offer a cool honeysuckle scent with hints of lemon and spice. A narcissus by other names may not smell as sweet. The scent of poet's narcissus (*N. poeticus*), for instance, has been described as "fecal."

Many of us have childhood recollections of forcing fragrant paperwhite bulbs (*N. papyraceus*) on the windowsill of a cool room. A shallow bowl without a drainage hole is filled halfway with gravel or pebbles; the paperwhite bulbs are placed on top, pointed end up;

and about ½ inch more gravel is added. The gravel is kept moist, and soon roots will appear—a fascinating process to witness, especially if the bulbs are planted in a clear glass bowl. In six weeks or so, the flowers will bloom.

If you think your recollection of sweet and spicy paperwhites has been sugarcoated over time, since you now find their scent unpleasant, it may not be a trick of your mind. Paperwhite varieties used to be imported from southern France, but according to some suppliers, Israeli hybrids with larger flowers have come to dominate the market. Many people find the scent of these hybrids objectionable: a musky combination of lily, tuberose, and boxwood, or even, to some noses, cat urine.

There are still some sweet varieties to hunt down—for instance, bicolor *N.* 'Grand Soleil d'Or' and *N.* 'Chinese Sacred Lily'.

Once forced, most spring-flowering bulbs cannot be made to bloom in pots again. Being spectacular the first time around just takes too much out of them. Cold-hardy bulbs *can* be planted in the garden once they've finished their indoor display; however, paperwhites, among the only spring bulbs that do not need to be pre-chilled, are tender and can be planted only in Zone 8 gardens and warmer.

OPPOSITE: Paperwhite narcissus forced indoors. ABOVE RIGHT: Daffodil small-cupped *Narcissus* 'Irish Coffee'. ABOVE LEFT: Sweetly fragrant *N. jonquilla* 'Sailboat'.

food have many options, from canning to freezing. But how do we preserve fragrance without building a laboratory in the basement? Few flowers retain their scent for very long after being dried, and I've never met a potpourri I liked. Finding ways to store the fragrant essences of plants has been a goal for nearly as long as fresh flowers, herbs, and spices have been used to scent the body and home.

Flower petals were pressed to squeeze out their oils, boiled for decoctions, steeped for infusions, immersed in oil, whipped into emollients, mixed with honey, and pounded into paste. Herb leaves, stems, and roots have been dried, burned, or ground into dust. Some of the earliest perfumes created by the ancient civilizations used a process (still practiced today) called *enfleurage*, in which flowers were placed on trays spread with rendered animal fat. The petals were replaced frequently as the grease absorbed their fragrance. The fat was then dissolved in alcohol and used, or distilled for essential oils, the purest concentrations of fragrant extracts.

About 5,000 years ago, the Mesopotamians had machines for steam-extracting the essential oils from plants. Steam caused herb leaves or flower petals to produce gases, which were then cooled and liquefied. Roses were the first plants to be commercially distilled for their fragrant oils. These oils were then dissolved in alcohol or diluted with vegetable oil or water, which, depending on the dilution, produced perfume, cologne, or the least concentrated, eau de toilette.

Perfumers describe the layers of a fragrance as "chords": the base, the heart, and the head.

Scents for perfume are characterized by seven descriptive "notes," most of which are botanical. The categories are floral, citrus, green, Oriental, leather, animal, cyphre, and aldehydic scents.

Floral scents can be derived from individual flowers or blends that are aptly called bouquets (like a nosegay of violets, or tussy-mussies of mixed flowers).

Citrus essences range from citron to tangerine. The origin of the species *Citrus medica,* the citron, is unknown, but it was the first citrus fruit to be cultivated according to records dating back to 4000 B.C. The citron or *etrog,* believed to have originally been imported from Persia, is one of the four revered species of Sukkot, the Jewish harvest festival of the tabernacles, and symbolized fertility (the others are palm, *lulav*; myrtle, *hadas*; and willow, *aravah*). The citron variety I grow indoors is *C. medica* 'Sarcodactylis', called, among other names, Buddha's hand. I rooted the plant from a cutting given to me by Laura Cadwallader, a gardening friend who grows the plant outdoors in San Antonio, Texas. The lemon-colored fruit has no juicy vesicles, just rind and pith, and resembles a distorted human hand with creepy fingers. The smell of the skin is not like a citrus blossom, or freshly cut rind, but has a distinctive, warm floral perfume that can and does fill a room.

Green to the perfumer is the smell of crushed leaves. These are the scents of fresh herbs such as rosemary and lavender, as well as pine needles and the smell of just-mown lawn.

ABOVE: Citrus smells are well known. The fruit of citron variety *Citrus medica* 'Sarcodactylus', Buddha's hand, scents a room with the light, sweet aroma of lemon and honey.

OPPOSITE: Despite the tuberose's ability to fill the house with fragrance, the essential oil made from the flowers is among the most expensive. It takes 3,600 pounds of *Polianthes tuberosa* blossoms to yield 1 pound of the pure distillate called "absolute." Garden variety 'The Pearl' with double flowers, shown.

BACK TO BASICS

A few major rose producers and most of the specialty mail-order rose nurseries offer "own-root" roses grown from cuttings. The smaller nurseries are your best bet when looking for hard-to-find varieties, particularly antique roses. Own-root rose plants are slower to mature, but do better for me.

Tom Carruth develops new varieties for Weeks Roses, a major California grower. Nearly a third of his company's roses are grown on their own roots (over a million plants in 2006). But he admits that demand has not spread quickly through the market.

I buy most of my roses from Antique Rose Emporium in Brenham, Texas. Their potted plants arrive in great condition thanks to ingenious packaging—a kind of corrugated cardboard origami.

The "secrets" to growing healthy roses are to give them an ample root run in rich soil, excellent drainage, no competition from other plants or weeds for 3 feet in every direction, mulch in summer, and winter protection, including mounding the soil up to a foot over the plants in cold climates. Roses further demand good air circulation, sunshine for no less than 10 hours a day in summer, and consistent moisture for the roots. Finally, you should not wet the leaves unless it is to wash them off in the morning when sunlight and a nice breeze will dry them off in 10 minutes or so.

Today's generation of gardeners looks for healthy, disease-resistant plants. We have no interest in using an arsenal of chemicals. One breakthrough came in 1999 with the appearance of 'Knock Out', a barely scented rose bred specifically for disease resistance by William Radler. 'Knock Out' has eye-jarring magenta flowers, but good marketing, good health, and continuous bloom made it the fastest-selling new rose in history, with 250,000 sold in 2000, 3.5 million in 2005.

But we gardeners also want fragrance. In 1996 Tom Carruth introduced a white and blood-red striped floribunda rose (one having numerous flowers on each stem) called 'Scentimental'. Here, at last, was a new rose with a spicy, old rose scent.

ABOVE: Fragrant striped rose 'Scentimental'.

Then there are the spice scents of *Oriental blends* typified by thick or heavy smells—incense, cinnamon, or sandalwood. Oriental blends may include the complex scent of the subshrub sweet fern (*Comptonia peregrina*), raisin and cinnamon with a touch of pine; the faint caramel fragrance of the Katsura tree (*Cercidiphyllum japonicum*) leaves in autumn; the anise smell of sweet pepperbush (*Clethra alnifolia*); the root-beer tang of sassafras (*Sassafras albidum*); and the cherry/wintergreen aroma of sweet birch (*Betula lenta*).

Leather/animal scents are nearly always derived from mammals (although some aroids, such as skunk cabbage, could be categorized here).

Cyphre (the French name for Cyprus) scents include honey-sweet smells such as that of littleleaf linden flowers (*Tilia cordata*) or the deep fragrance of sweet alyssum (*Lobularia maritima*). Sometimes there is also a hint of chlorine—for example, the cloying, honey-and-bleach odor associated with privet flowers (*Ligustrum* species).

Aldehydes are colorless, volatile liquids, which in their molecular structure fall between alcohols and acids. Natural aldehydic scents are found in flowers with somewhat chemical odors such as the Carolina allspice shrub described by friends as smelling like lacquer thinner. Most aldehydes are synthetic today. The ultrachic, ultramodern perfume Chanel No. 5, launched in 1921, was one of the first fragrances to include artificial aldehydes.

"Artificial" sounds cheap, like artificial flavors, but some of these compounds are very expensive, costing more than their botanical counterparts. According to professional "noses," the synthetics may be stabler—and since high prices are part of the cachet of designer perfumes, the cost of artificial scents is rarely an issue.

Today synthetic scents are commonly used in perfume making, while many organic essential oils are relegated to bath and body products such as high-priced soaps and shampoos. That is, however, not always the case. Some botanicals are inimitable and, due to rarity or the amounts needed for extraction, very expensive.

The essence tuberose from the flower of *Polianthes tuberosa* (a.k.a. *Tuberosa polianthes* and *Agave polianthes*) is used in many designer fragrances—and contributes significantly to their high prices. It takes 3,600 pounds of tuberose blossoms, at several hundred dollars a pound, to produce 1 pound of pure tuberose oil, or "absolute."

Native to Mexico (where it is known as *omixochitl*, "bone flower," for the color of the blossoms), the tuberose is a relative of the succulent agaves (family Agavaceae). The tubers first reached Europe in 1594 and have been farmed commercially near Grasse, France, ever since. Grasse is the center of perfume production in France and home to the rose fields—farms where flowers for scent and essential oils are grown. The two old roses cultivated there for perfumes are commercially known as *rose bulgare* (*Rosa damascena*) and *rose de mai* (*R. centifolia*).

TOP TO BOTTOM: Sweet pepper bush (*C. alnifolia* 'Ruby Spice') has an anise fragrance. Little leaf linden trees (*Tilia cordata*) have a cloying honey scent. Fragrant gallica roses, in cultivation as early as 1200 B.C., include the variety 'Complicata'.

TOO LITTLE OF A GOOD THING

While walking through the garden with my neighbor Jill Hagler, who came of age during the 1980s, I had the pleasure of introducing her to one of my favorite roses, a charming medium pink flower that was growing on the property when I bought it. I knew it was an old variety, but it took quite a bit of detective work to discover its name. Unlike the modern hybrid tea roses that have flowers throughout the season, this rose blooms only once for about a month. The buds are pointed, and the rose, which has a flat face when fully open, measures a little over 2 inches across. The plant is rarely diseased, begins to bloom a few weeks before the Japanese beetles emerge, and tolerates a bit of shade, a coveted attribute in roses. The shrub is upright and twiggy, and it used to grow among tall weeds, but early on, I replaced those with hydrangeas, deutzia, *Amsonia hubrectii*, columbines, and heat-tolerant New Zealand delphiniums grown from seed. The best I can come up with is that this rose is 'Petite de Hollande', a variety some sources list as being introduced prior to 1791.

I picked one of the roses and gave it to Jill, who held it to her nose and announced, "It smells like soap." Her observation made me realize that she had never met an old rose before, an antique European variety grown before the introduction of the hybrid teas. "Actually," I told her, "it's the other way around. Soap smells like the rose."

The first thing everyone does when he or she meets a rose is smell it. The fragrance we've come to associate with these flowers is often a blend of tropical fruits and a whiff of a just-opened tin of loose tea. That is the scent of roses with European and Chinese blood—the hybrid teas first introduced in 1867. When gardeners picture a "rose," they may think of the yellow or pink blossoms, or the tropical color blends and sunset hues of hybrid teas. These flowers—grown on the new introductions, promoted with great fanfare by the major growers, well publicized—open into plump urn-shaped blossoms with high centers and large, separate petals that roll outward at the edges. When most *Americans* think of a rose, they picture the hybrid teas, long-stemmed, high-priced, and *red*.

This generalized image of a red rose originated with a plant that was imported into the United States in the 1880s. The French immigrant was named 'Madame Ferdinand Jamin'. She was remarkable, bearing an enormous fat bud on a stem that, when greenhouse-grown, could reach 6 feet. The color was carmine, claret, deep pink, and red, and the flower was very fragrant. The rose had not done well in its homeland—too difficult to grow in cool summer climates—and the variety would certainly have been banished to the compost heap here as well if not for a stroke of marketing genius. The Field Bros. nursery changed the rose's name to 'American Beauty', and thereby guaranteed its future. Any flower producer who could master its cultivation as a cut flower could make his or her fortune, and did.

OPPOSITE: One of the roses grown for essential oil in the fields of Grasse, France, is called *rose de mai* (*Rosa centifolia*). A wonderfully fragrant small-flowered *R. centifolia* variety grew in my garden when I bought the place, and through research, I've discovered that it could be 'Petite de Hollande', which may date from 1791.

In an 1887 wholesale catalog, the roses were listed as selling for 50 cents apiece, and they retailed for between $1 and $2—the equivalent of a full day's pay.

The impact of 'American Beauty' on cut-flower fashion and flower arranging is still being felt today. Before the appearance of 'American Beauty', multistemmed roses were arranged in hemispheric compositions in low bowls. But after the introduction of 'American Beauty', long-stemmed roses in tall vases became vogue. Soon rose breeders began producing knockoffs that were easier to grow, but all were collectively referred to as 'American Beauty'.

By the middle of the 20th century, most rose varieties in America had long stems; could stand up to forcing in greenhouses, cutting, packing, and year-round shipping—in or out of water; and would hold up under the rigor of amateur flower-arranging competitions. These stylish hybrids won awards and the seal of approval from rose societies for good "petal substance." So smitten were people by the ever newer roses, no one seemed to notice that one of the most beloved characteristics of roses such as 'Madame Ferdinand Jamin' was disappearing: scent.

The poet and environmental science essayist Diane Ackerman reported in her book *A Natural History of the Senses* (1990) that fragrance is a recessive gene. In breeding for long-lasting, long-stemmed cut flowers for arranging, hybridizers lost scent. I also speculate that when a rose (or any other flower) emits a fragrance, it is actually giving some of itself away as molecules flowing into the air. So, when roses are bred with sturdy, almost leathery petals that do not disintegrate quickly, they hold on to their molecules. There is nothing to share with a willing nose.

give peace a chance

Besides fragrance, another characteristic of the old roses was lost during the years of intensive breeding: good health. Initial crosses may produce hybrid vigor, or *heterosis*, but back-breeding siblings may lead to inbreeding depression and a compounding of weak genes, perhaps a problem with the original 'American Beauty'. However, back in the 1950s, hybrid vigor was rarely a consideration for gardeners who thought it a normal practice to spray fungicides and pesticides weekly; after all, we were living better through chemistry. Every weekend began with the same chores: mow the lawn, spray the roses—to stave off disease and nip insect infestations in the bud, as it were.

Some hybrid varieties grow so poorly—with weak roots and therefore spindly growth that is easy prey for pests—that they cannot survive unless they are grafted to a stronger plant's roots. This is one reason you'll find that most roses sold today are grafted. But the main reason growers graft buds of a desired rose variety onto an understock or rootstock of another is to produce as many good-size clones (genetically identical plants) as fast as possible.

ABOVE: When most people think of a rose, they picture a long-stemmed red flower—a conventional notion that originated with a French rose 'Madame Ferdinand Jamin', which in a stroke of marketing genius was renamed 'American Beauty'. In the 1880s, one rose retailed for the equivalent of an average day's pay.

PLANT 'EM IF YOU'VE GOT 'EM

Nicotiana alata hybrids, most often crosses between *N. × sanderae* and *N. alata,* smell strongest at dusk, when they release a deep, heavy aroma of lilies, clove, vanilla, and winter jasmine. Although nicotiana plants behave as if they were annuals (growing from seed, blooming, setting seed, and withering at the end of the season), they are perennials in Zone 8 and warmer.

Every flower makes scores of seeds, and depending on the climate, a few plants may show up the next year from self-sown seed. The resulting generation will not look exactly like the plants they came from, and in subsequent years new plants' flowers bloom in a dirty mauve color. Of course, this uncommon shade is right up my alley, and I've been collecting seeds from some of the darkest "mutts" to sow the following spring.

When my plants produced a nut-brown variant, I decided I had a variety worth cloning—ensuring future generations with same-colored flowers. In the fall, I dug up two of the choicest brown-flowered plants and trimmed the top green growth to about an inch or two. I washed the roots clean, wrapped the plants loosely in barely damp sphagnum moss, and slipped them into clean plastic bags in the refrigerator. In March, one got potted and went to a sunny window. The other was made into root cuttings.

Nicotiana is easy to propagate from 3-inch-long sections of roots. I cut them with a single-edged razor blade and keep the thickest, whitest sections. The most important thing is to maintain polarity: the skyward end up, and earth end down. I fill a 6-inch plastic pot with moistened, soilless potting mix and poke five to ten holes in the medium with a pencil and lower a cutting into each hole, so the skyward end is flush with the surface. I sprinkle a thin layer of very coarse sand or chicken grit on top, put my pots in a sunny window, and soon shoots appear. After all danger of frost has passed, and following a few weeks of helping the plants acclimatize outdoors, I can set them into the garden.

ABOVE: Most rose varieties today are budded—grafted to another rose's roots, and sold bare-root.

OPPOSITE, CLOCKWISE FROM TOP LEFT: The common rootstock for budded roses in the United States is 'Dr. Huey', a climber that has come up in my garden when the purchased top growth variety died.

'Peace', the hybrid tea rose, is named for the end of World War II.

'Constance Spry', the first so-called English rose, was introduced by David Austin in 1963.

One David Austin shrub rose, 'Graham Thomas', named for the late horticulturist, combines the form of antique roses with the color and reblooming characteristics of modern roses.

Unfortunately, there are other drawbacks to the grafted rose. The bud union—where the grafted variety (the scion) joins the rootstock—is susceptible to damage during digging, shipping, and planting. But disease and hardiness are the bigger problems. For decades, the understock used for grafting was infected with viruses that were transmitted to the scion buds. Growers claim that this is no longer a problem; however, as far as cold tolerance, if the desirable flowering variety on top is reported to be hardy to USDA Zone 2 or even Zone 4, it might not survive the winter, given the fact that the understock, most often *Rosa* 'Dr. Huey', is hardy only to Zone 6 (the most optimistic estimates claim Zone 5). Because of this, whenever I plant a grafted rose, I bury the bud union 2 inches below the soil surface in my Zone 6 garden, and I suggest another inch deeper for every zone colder. If I'm lucky, the chosen variety will produce its own roots above the bud union and secure itself into the soil without help from the dear old doc.

But 'Dr. Huey' might also send up shoots of his own from below the bud union, which gives rise to an often-heard comment, "My rose reverted. I planted a yellow and pink 'Peace', but the next year, it bloomed red." The 'Peace' rose did not revert, it died, and 'Dr. Huey' took its place.

in with the old

Over the last 20 years or so, several rose hybrids that capture the best qualities of the antique varieties, and the best of the newer roses as well, have appeared on the market. The fragrances of these hybrids are reminiscent of both old and new roses; some have the bath-powder scent of old-fashioned roses, and others, the fruit and tea aromas of the modern hybrid teas. Unlike the antique roses that bloom only once each season, most of these newer plants rebloom like the hybrid teas. Many of the plants have the disease resistance of the healthier old roses and their bushy habit, but the flower colors include the warm shades such as apricot, orange, and yellow found in the modern varieties. These plants are the "English roses," an unofficial category of "shrub roses" named by their creator, David Austin.

Like many entrepreneurs, David Austin recognized a need and filled it. As a teenager in the 1940s, he came across the book *Old Garden Roses* by Edward Bunyard. The antique roses in the book—white-, pink-, or red-flowered species and strains of gallicas, damasks, and albas—had nearly disappeared from gardens at that time. The book gave Austin the idea of crossing the rugged old varieties with "modern" ones that came on the market after the introduction of the first hybrid tea rose, 'La France', in 1867.

In 1963, Austin introduced his first variety, 'Constance Spry', a climber that blooms just once a year. I've seen a spectacular specimen of this rose climbing a wall, in full sun, covered with a thousand double pink roses. I have 'Constance Spry' planted behind the south-facing wall of the gravel garden, and I'm training it

to grow up through a red-leaved peach tree and a double pink lilac shrub. Roses resent crowding, and many would die in that situation. The 'Constance Spry' plant is growing slowly, and blooming. Despite being crowded, in some shade, and with air circulation blocked by the wall, the plant is disease-free.

Austin crossed 'Constance Spry' with a few of his next varieties, among them 'Chianti' in 1967 and 'Shropshire Lass' in 1968, and the results were repeat-blooming roses. There have been many triumphs since these first repeat-blooming roses appeared. One of the most popular and enduring creations debuted at the Chelsea Flower Show in 1983, the gallant, sunny yellow 'Graham Thomas', named for the late rose expert, writer, and former director of gardens for England's National Trust. Since that time, Austin has introduced more than 150 new roses.

I don't remember the first English rose I ever saw, but I remember the first one I smelled: 'Abraham Darby' (1985). I found the fragrance delicious—the familiar scent of an antique rose, dust and jasmine, but layered with fruity guava and tea. I've been smelling roses for a long time, and I can honestly say the Austin roses, which practically sell themselves (more than 1.2 million plants were shipped to markets in 2005), do not disappoint.

I should pose a caveat, here, or a disclaimer. It is hard to generalize about rose vigor and health, since so much depends on the immediate environment. In roses, as in real estate, it is often a matter of location, location, location.

CREATURES OF THE NIGHT

The sweetly scented roses prefer sunny days, when their colorful flowers are shown off to best effect. These plants descended from pollen-laden ancestors that pleased

ABOVE, LEFT TO RIGHT: Perhaps best of all, the Austin roses, like 'Abraham Darby', are fragrant.

Many plants are pollinated by night creatures, even petunias, which become clove-scented at dusk.

Moonflower does not even open until 5:00 P.M., when you can actually watch it quickly unfurl.

OPPOSITE, TOP TO BOTTOM: Moonflower's cousins include varieties of *Brugmansia*, most of which smell like winter-green, except the varie-gated white-flowered one that hints of cake batter.

Tobacco, including *Nicotiana mutabilis*, with mutable flower colors from white to pink to rose, is a *Solanum* cousin.

The species *N. sylvestris* has 4- to 5-inch-long flaring white flowers.

the bees, but fancy double flowers bred by hybridizers may hold empty promises: they often have little nectar to share. Scores of other garden flowers are also wonderfully fragrant, yet these plants offer nothing for the bees either: they do not even begin to fill the air with scent until after the bees have flown home to their hives to sleep.

Evening is when other pollinators are just starting to stir, and when I make my rounds of the night-scented flowers. The reason the flowers evolved to smell at night, and why their pollinators emerge only then, is another curious example of convergent evolution. Which came first, evening scent or nocturnal pollinators? I can guess that there was less competition at night for food (nectar), but there may be other issues at play. Perhaps some pollinators dehydrate in the heat of the day, so they stay undercover until the sun sets and the temperatures cool. They may have evolved to be active at night because their potential predators were not. As for the flowers, why reveal blooms during the day and waste pollen if your primary visitor is asleep? It is interesting to speculate while I am sampling some of the surprises of the evening garden.

Four-o'clocks are aptly named for the time their flowers open. And at around 5:00 P.M., the moonflower begins to unfurl. If you are lucky enough to be present for the opening of this morning glory relative, you can witness its pointed bud untwisting into a large pentagonal flower right before your eyes. In many cases, the night-scented flowers evolved to be white and large, like the luminous moonflower, to reflect moonlight, which makes the plants easy to find in the dark.

The all-too-common petunia is often shunned by jaded gardeners, but it can be held in higher regard once its evening fragrance is sampled. At dusk petunias release a heady, deep scent of marshmallow, lily, and clove. Varieties that most closely resemble species, ones that have not been overbred but have white or pale lavender flowers, seem to smell strongest.

Many evening-scented plants, including the petunias, are members of the nightshade family (Solanacaea), which comprises genera from Central and South America such as tropical tomatoes, potatoes, eggplant, and peppers. The name *nightshade*—as in "deadly nightshade," *Atropa belladonna*—is a tipoff that these plants could be poisonous. Even the leaves of tomatoes can be toxic. *Nicotiana*, as its name suggests, is the source of tobacco, so it is no wonder that cigarette smoke has unsafe properties.

Nicotiana tabacum is the species grown, dried, and rolled into cigarettes, but there are nearly 70 other members of the genus, several of which are familiar garden plants and others that should be. For example, *N. mutabilis* is an easy-to-grow species with "mutable" flower colors from dark pink to white—on the same plant at the same time. *N. sylvestris* bears 4- to 5-inch-long, downward-facing white tubes at the top of 3- to 4-foot-tall plants. *N. langsdorffii* grows to less than 2 feet and bears 1-inch elongated chartreuse bells—not much of a show on their own, but the

display can be striking when planted en masse, and, for example, against a dark background such as a yew hedge.

Most gardeners grow *Nicotiana* strains and hybrids, the vividly colored varieties in the Sensation Series or the Nicki Series hybrids—stumpy plants with red, pink, or white flowers—being the most popular. Needless to say, these less-fragrant, brightly colored hybrids look out of place to me, unless one is trying his or her hand at Victorian carpet bedding or planting a traffic island at the airport parking lot. However, I have to admit to one exception: 'Nicki Lime', a plant that sports apple green flowers and manages to look somewhat like it might actually be a creation of nature.

The extremely ornamental cousins of the flowering tobacco can make dramatic statements in the summer garden. *Solanum* species are noteworthy for their threat-

ABOVE LEFT: *Solanum quitoense* has spines on the veins of its leaves, warning that this plant, like most pepper family members, is poisonous if eaten.

ABOVE: A *Solanum* cousin is angel's trumpet, *Brugmansia* 'Charles Grimaldi', with flowers nearly a foot long.

ABOVE RIGHT: Annual or short-lived perennial datura, thorn apple or locoweed, is closely related to the angel's trumpet, and even more toxic. The selection *Datura metel* 'Double Purple' bears a large, exquisitely complex flower.

ening spines brandished on giant leaves. *Datura* species are known by such common names as jimsonweed, thorn apple, and locoweed (eating any part of the plant may produce hallucinations, drive you crazy, or kill you). One selection of *D. metel* 'Double Purple' bears flowers that look like ice cream cones filled with meringue and dipped in blackberry syrup. Most *Datura* behave like annuals, producing flowers continuously and then fruits in one season.

Datura's very close relative is *Brugmansia*, called angels' trumpets, which is poisonous as well (eat some and expect the angel Gabriel's blaring call to heaven). The brugmansia is more like a tree than the shrubby datura. The notion that about half of the brugmansia varieties bloom with the new moon and the others with the full moon seems to be a myth, although most do bloom in waves with a resting period

ABOVE AND LEFT:
The most extraordinary orchid cactus is the night-blooming cereus (*Epiphyllum oxypetalum*), which on one night in the late summer, begins to unfurl from a dangling bud. Within an hour or so, depending on the temperature, the flower is fully open, and a sweet perfume of wintergreen fills the air. A century ago, the event was cause for neighbors to gather on the front porch to watch the event. By morning, the flower was closed. In its homeland of the West Indies, pollinating bats bury their faces in anthers, licking nectar from the throat of the blossom.

in between when new buds develop. One, however, *B.* × *candida* 'Shredded White', seems to bloom continuously. Each blossom first opens looking like a trumpet, and then a second twisted inner "flower" develops. The hybrids are not grown from seed but are propagated vegetatively from cuttings.

Unlike datura flowers that usually face upward, toward the viewer, brugmansia blossoms tend to hang down. The angel's trumpets may be 12 inches long or more, in white, lemon yellow, or deep pink to orange with tints in between; some flowers have bicolor shadings, and all are evening fragrant, most smelling like pepsin, or a light to heavy wintergreen fragrance. The white-flowered blossoms of the variegated *B. suaveolens* 'Variegata', however, smell like yellow cake batter.

opening night

Early in the last century, people enjoyed an annual ritual during the waning days of summer. On one night, and only one night, neighbors would gather on the porch, sip lemonade, and witness the unfurling buds of the night-blooming cereus (*Epiphyllum oxypetalum*), a jungle cactus originating in Mexico and the West Indies. Two weeks earlier, brownish pointed buds would have appeared, growing larger every day until they reached the size of navel oranges dangling from 12-inch-long, S-shaped floral tubes. By then, it was clear that the blessed event was at hand. One afternoon, the petals would begin to open slightly, and the word was sent out to the guests. It was opening night!

The flowers open between 8:00 P.M. and 10:00 P.M., and depending on the temperature, they take a half hour to four hours to spread to the width of a dinner plate. On hot summer nights, they open fast enough to see them move. Then, the fragrance fills the air. Once you've witnessed such a glorious event, it's easy to understand why this once-a-year experience became a ritual to be shared with friends and family.

In general, the night-blooming cereus needs to be pot-bound to bloom, to have its roots undisturbed, and to have a period of dormancy, which in my climate means to keep it lean (do not feed the plant), cool, and dry in winter. I've grown this plant off and on since I was a teenager—putting up with both its lanky and often homely flat stems and pots that toppled over and broke under the top-heavy plant's weight. These broken pots frustratingly meant repotting, an act that might set the plant back in its blooming cycle to square one.

In order to get an old plant back in blooming shape for this book, I braced the pot with bricks and tied the gangly limbs to a central stake; then in spring, I repotted it into a container *just one* size larger. Once the danger of frost had passed in May, I moved the plant outdoors to the west-facing porch and watered it, allowing the top inch or so of soil to dry before drenching it again. New green shoots pushed from old stems and branched into sets of flat leaves. By July, the fresh

growth had stopped and the tissues hardened. While the clock ticked louder toward summer's end, flower buds were appearing.

As the big night approached, I enlisted a friend to keep watch when I had to be in Brooklyn, unable to sit vigil. Finally, I got the call. "Are the tips of the petals fraying, opening slightly?" I asked. "Have they moved since you've been there? Is there a tiny opening at the tip? Should I get in the car? Can you e-mail me a digital image?" I realize now how much this is to ask of any friend, but I'd been waiting three years for this moment to arrive.

My friend sent me the photo of the cereus and I jumped in my car to drive the 60 miles, fully prepared to play Lamaze coach. I arrived at 10:00 P.M., which thankfully was not too late; in fact, the relatively cool night temperature had slowed the process, and one of the buds had yet to completely open. I set up the lights and cameras and settled in for what could have been hours of labor. It was around midnight that I took the picture you see here. It took being dry, cool, and filling a small pot with roots to begin the process, but it seems that the cereus plant enjoyed this kind of tough love. The next night, as my friend and I ate a celebratory dinner, it wasn't the effort expended we talked about but the beauty and drama of the timeless spectacle.

ABOVE, FROM LEFT: The calla lily, *Zantedeschia aethiopica*, has the quintessential aroid inflorescence with a spathe and central spadix.

The balloonlike flower bud of a *Stapelia*, the starfish flower. When ready to open, the tip untwists, and bud splits along seams to reveal a five-pointed star.

ABOVE, FROM LEFT: The open *Stapelia gigantea* flower has markings that make it look like carrion to pollinators such as flies. The odor, too, mimics the smell of rotting flesh.

Berkeley, California, sculptor Marcia Donahue created a ceramic interpretation of an aroid inflorescence.

THE NOSE KNOWS

Some of the most fragrant plants delight me in the evening, others in the warm sunlight in the middle of the day. While I agree that there are plants that do not smell so great, at least not to us humans, I can also appreciate these stinky plants and their efforts to attract animals for pollination or to disseminate seeds. Species in the genera *Stapelia* and *Huernia* have starfishlike flowers that look and also smell like something washed up on the beach and left in the sun. These plants are pollinated by flies, and when a flower on mine opens, I have to take a photo immediately, before flies lay their eggs on the putrid blossom.

The flesh surrounding a female ginkgo's seed has a nauseating odor, which is why only male plants are ordered for street tree planting. Somehow or other, a few girls slip onto the truck and get planted, to the regret of neighbors a decade later—and to the delight of a few urban Asians, who consider the washed seeds a delicacy.

The smelly-plant-family award, however, should probably go to the aroids, genera in the family Araceae. Some aroids flower when the ground is thawing in late winter, and their scent mimics the odor of carrion. This is an ingenious adaptation, since it's quite likely that animals that didn't survive the winter are beginning to thaw and

sending out a similar scent. The smell attracts beetles and flies looking for a suitable spot to lay their eggs. Other aroids bloom later, when baby animals might meet with unfortunate ends and their carcasses attract insects looking for food and a place to brood. Some of the aroids mimic the scents of those seasonal casualties.

Aroids are soft-tissue herbaceous plants, encompassing some 110 genera and 1,800 species, many of which grow from rhizomes or tubers. They can be found in tropical, subtropical, warm-temperate, and temperate regions of the world. Aroids are identified by their floral structures: a spadix, a central flower-covered inflorescence, usually a spike, and a spathe, a modified leaf that either forms an attracting foil for the spadix (*Anthurium,* for example) or wraps around it (*Caladium*). Many aroids have defensive calcium oxalate crystals (needlelike raphides) that are supposed to keep herbivores at bay (they did not stop the black bear from eating my garden's precious *Arisaema ringens,* however).

The aroid *Dracunculus vulgaris* has been called dragon arum or voodoo lily. The 2006 Plant Delights Nursery catalog described the inflorescence as looking like a ". . . purple, ruffled vase . . . from the center of which emerges a fleshy appendage resembling an upside-down purple carrot." Tony Avent, co-owner of Plant Delights, recommends, "Hold the phone . . . hold your nose . . . cover your eyes . . . the dazzling Viagra lily is ready to flower."

Most of the aroids we come in contact with are tropical, like the houseplant philodendron. Avent also sells tropical species for growing outdoors in summer and wintering indoors, either as dormant tubers or in a sunroom or greenhouse. The corpse flower, *Amorphophallus titanum,* is the world's tallest flower and the largest single-leaved plant; its thick, hollow, turgid, dappled "trunk" can stretch up to 12 feet tall. This curiosity makes front-page news whenever it blooms at U.S. botanical gardens.

I grow the 4-foot-tall *Amorphophallus konjac* (formerly *A. rivieri*) in a large container, where its potato-like tuber may grow to the size of a grapefruit. When the plant blooms, in mid- to late winter, a slender spike emerges out of the pot as a lurid, organ-meat-colored, leopard-spotted spear unfurls; and then it begins to smell. If it is too cold to take the plant outdoors (below 55 degrees F), I have to give it its own room in the house.

After the inflorescence fades, a spear emerges from the pot that looks like a green and silver spotted baseball bat and grows larger and taller, up to 4 feet, before it too begins to unfurl. Skinny, green, lobed leaflets appear and elongate into a three-part, feathery pinnate leaf. All of this sexy action should not be too surprising from a plant whose generic name *Amorphophallus* could be translated as "shape-shifting penis."

To be fair, the tropical aroids are not all shocking, although they are flamboyant. And the ones we're most likely to grow for summer foliage interest do not bloom often or have malodorous foliage. Caladiums and elephant's ear (*Colocasia esculenta*) were frequent guests of honor in Victorian gardens, and they are once

ABOVE: Dwarf calla lilies now come in a variety of colors.

OPPOSITE, CLOCKWISE FROM TOP LEFT: The inflorescence of *Amorphophallus konjac* (syn. *A. rivieri,* devil's tongue) smells so foul that if it blooms in winter, I have to give it its own room.

A close-up shows the white male flower buds. The tuber of the plant is a food source in Yunnan and Sichuan, and has a medicinal polysaccharide that is said to reduce total cholesterol and blood glucose for treating diabetes and leading to weight loss.

This is the flowering structure of *Colocasia esculenta* 'Black Magic'.

The aubergine leaves of the 5-foot-tall black taro with an *Abutilon,* flowering maple. Although I dig up the tubers to store dry over winter, red color (anthocyanins) may lead to cold protection, and with a mulch, the dormant underground tubers may survive to 0°F.

ABOVE: The flowering structures of skunk cabbage (*Symplocarpus foetidus*) attract pollinators and protect flowers in the icy winter by metabolizing starch and raising the spathe's interior temperature up to 70°F.

OPPOSITE: Leafy skunk cabbage plants are in their natural habitat in moist woodland clearings.

again back in fashion. Because of this renewed interest, gardeners have many varieties from which to choose, including the related large-leaved varieties from the genera *Alocasia* and *Xanthosoma*.

The florists' calla lily, *Zantedeschia aethiopica*, is a semiaquatic aroid that is grown for its flower, the familiar pure white spadix and spathe. There are also varieties available in stunning shades of deep maroon, orange, red, and yellow. To the best of my knowledge, none of these plants smell bad, in or out of flower. But even if they did, their junglelike contribution to the garden *might* make it worth putting up with the temporary unpleasantness of the odors.

a skunk by any other name

While lecturing to members of the New England Wild Flower Society in Framingham, Massachusetts, some years back, I mentioned that I liked the American native aroid we know as skunk cabbage (*Symplocarpus foetidus*). Several members of the audience promptly offered me as much as I could remove from their woodlands, adding that they'd happily provide the spade. It seems the humble skunk cabbage remains an underappreciated wildflower.

Is it the aroid's common name? But the odor is the source of half of the common name; the plant's appearance suggests the second half. Is it because the flower colors are muted, or that they bloom too early for most wildflower enthusiasts to ever see? Perhaps the plants are too difficult to get to in marshy spots where gardeners fear to tread. Or is it the smell? I don't think the plants smell all that much unless the foliage is bruised, and then it is not so unpleasant—in fleeting doses.

I'm used to looking for rarely noticed plants, and I tend to find the subtle and even bizarre much more alluring than a bed full of overblown identical red tulips. Apparently, I'm not alone. Henry David Thoreau took note of the skunk cabbage's flowers and had an appreciation for them as well. In his March 16, 1860, journal entry he wrote, "I examine the skunk cabbage, now generally and abundantly in bloom. All that you see is a stout beaked hood just rising above the dead brown grass in the springy ground. The single enveloping leaf, or 'spathe,' is all the flower that you see commonly, and those are as variously colored as tulips."

The stiff spathes open a few weeks before the foliage begins to grow, and they range in color from eggplant purple to mustard yellow, streaked or splashed with maroon or flaxen. In clusters of two or three, the hooded spathes look like a caucus of monks. Though subtle, the spathes are easy to spot if there has been a light snowfall. These wetlanders generate heat as they convert starch stored in their thick root to sugar, and this heat melts a circle around the spathe, marking the skunk cabbage's appearance. Over the two-week period when the tiny flowers on the spadix bear pollen, the temperature within the spathe can be as much as 40 degrees warmer than the surrounding air—up to 72 degrees F.

Why does the skunk cabbage blossom heat up? Sex. In early spring, before dormant bees rouse, flies are awake, and the plants attract more pollinators with the scent of rotting meat than with honey. A fly looking for a place to lay its eggs—on a dead bird or mouse perhaps—might be drawn to the smell rising in a vortex of warmed air above a colony of skunk cabbage plants. I suspect that the warmth also protects the opening flowers and ripe pollen from severe cold, and that insects such as beetles might creep into the spathe to find warmth and shelter, conveniently pollinating the tiny flowers at the same time.

The skunk cabbage's flowers begin to fade a few weeks after they appear, and the spathes shrivel as the young leaves expand, quickly growing as much as 2 feet long and 1 foot across.

Two related plants, also called skunk cabbages, are inarguably attractive. Both are in the genus *Lysichiton. L. americanus,* native to the Pacific Northwest of the United States, bears a showy yellow spathe, while *L. camtschatcensis,* from Japan, reveals a gorgeous white spathe. These plants, close relatives living an ocean apart, provide evidence in support of the theory of continental drift, when the once connected tectonic plates of the world split apart—separating the islands of Japan from the West Coast of North America. The *Lysichiton,* like wild gingers, Solomon's seal, and mayapples, for instance, lived together thousands of years ago, and they survived the breakup of Pangaea to evolve independently, but as analogous species.

The Pacific Northwestern and Japanese *Lysichiton* bear 10-inch-tall spathes that appear to have been carved out of wax. In my garden, these plants, grown from seedlings, took about three years to produce their first 3-inch-tall flowers, which have become larger and more numerous as the years have passed. After the flowers fade, paddle-shaped leaves emerge, growing up to 3 feet tall on mature plants. From time to time, these lovely species can be found in nursery catalogs.

To the best of my knowledge, the Eastern North American skunk cabbage that grows on my property (where it has very likely grown for thousands of years) is never offered for sale, but I have grown some from collected seeds. One thing about a moist, boggy spot—the so-called waste places—is that it is the last to be cleared or developed and therefore may have very old colonies of plants.

I have tagged two plants that had the most interesting flower colors so I could watch them and see whether the color variances are environmental or inherent to the individuals. If they keep their colors from year to year, deepest purple with yellow streaks, and yellow ocher with purple splashes, who knows, perhaps they might turn into interesting garden plants worthy of propagation. I don't condone moving these plants from the wild places where they grow, but if I can find a way to communicate what I see in the humble skunk cabbages to others, maybe they will come to respect them, and respect their wetland homes, as well.

PART THREE

elegant
design

No one has to be told flowers are beautiful; we seem to know that from birth. We are similarly drawn to paintings and sculpture and even architecture, much of which has been inspired by the beauty found in nature. These irresistible works of art share a remarkable commonality with plants and flowers, one that may also trigger an immediate, subliminal attraction. The more I learned about the incredible patterns that appear throughout art and nature, the more I had to know. I never imagined that the arrangement of each leaf, flower bud, and petal of nearly every plant on Earth would lead me on a journey that took me to the chambers of a Renaissance mathematician, further back to ancient Greece, and then home again to the garden.

OPPOSITE: The aggregation of bracts on the dry fruits of globe thistle (*Echinops ritro*) after the flowers fade.

AMAZING GRACE

From the time images of plants were drawn on cave walls, to modern interpretations in interior and industrial design, botanical forms have been considered nature's most exquisite inspirations. Architectural adornments, pottery design, wall covering and textiles, paintings and sculpture, private and public gardens—all have been influenced by the beauty, structure, and form found in the natural world.

Leonardo da Vinci, the visionary artist, designer, and scientist who predicted manned flying machines and demystified the human body, was also enthralled by the structure of plants, and he studied the arrangement of leaves around a stem. Each leaf, he noted, appeared in regular, measurable, and predictable order; Leonardo surmised that this "screw axis" benefited the plant and aided its ability to thrive. He was right, but his conclusions based on his observations do not tell the whole story.

Phyllotaxis, the study of leaf arrangement, has teased out a more complete explanation of this miracle in plant design, with the aid of a numerical formula that was recorded more than 900 years ago—a formula that applies to plants, nautilus shells, our very own fingerprints, and even the universe.

Complicated math equations were not what I was hoping to find when I went in search of answers to my questions about the patterns of spirals, whorls, and arcs I found on virtually every plant in the garden. But find equations I did, along with an intriguing connection between the patterns I investigated in plants and those found in art, architecture, and design.

Realizing that nature, art, and science are all linked shouldn't be all that surprising to a gardener—we know of such miracles occurring in our backyards and window boxes every day. But knowing more about these phenomena creates a deeper understanding. If you're anything like I am, you'll find that learning about these connections will change the way you look at plants, forever.

ANATOMY OF AN INSPIRATION

Genealogy is nearly as popular a "sport" these days as scrapbooking. If I apply the principles of genealogy to plants and learn who is in whose family, I can make some useful assumptions. This is more than a trivial pursuit; it is an exploration into the genius of nature, and it can provide insight into plant culture.

When I see a flower with five petals, whether a sprawling cotoneaster or an ancient apple tree, I love to speculate and investigate how these different plants might be related. Although the flowers of the cotoneaster and apple tree vary in size, each of the five petals radiates from a central boss, a button of fuzzy anthers. In fact, this common geometry can be found in the blossoms of the apple, cotoneaster, pear, quince, hawthorn, mountain ash, spirea, *Hypericum*, ninebark, almond, and cherry—plants that are *all in the family*, that family being rose or Rosaceae.

Once I've identified the family to which the plant belongs, I begin to speculate as to how the plants might benefit from similar treatment in the garden. I know, for instance, that rose family members like a lot of sunlight, are susceptible to certain diseases and insect attacks, and that many are deer candy. Plants in the *Berberis* family, Berberidaceae, on the other hand, are rarely if ever eaten by deer, and these include the woodland mayapple, the winter-flowering *Mahonia*, and the shade-tolerant ground cover *Epimedium*. I know that plants in the family Euphorbiaceae often have milky sap that may irritate my skin, so I should wear gloves when dividing them.

Species in the lily family, Lilaceae—which includes lilies, asparagus, yucca, hyacinth, and hosta—may produce offsets, small plants that grow along the bulb or stem of the parent plant, and have flower parts in sets of three. Flowers with four petals arranged like a plus sign are often crucifers (a word that shares the same root with *crucifix*) and in the family Brassicaceae. Included in this family are spring ornamentals such as *Arabis, Aubrieta, Cardamine,* and *Hesperis* as well as ornamental kale and the giant flowering cabbage cousin *Crambe*, which explodes into a cloud of baby's-breath-like blossoms in early summer. Edible plants like Brussels sprouts, cauliflower, broccoli, and horseradish are all brassicas, along with some stubborn self-sowing weeds, the mustards and cresses.

The florist's flower called stock (*Matthiola incana*) is a brassica, and I know I'm in for trouble if I leave it or other flowers in the family in a vase without recutting them and changing the water daily. Sauerkraut has nothing on these stinkers.

LEFT: Spirals are common in plants, from unfurling pinnae (leaflets, from the Latin for "feather") on a giant *Cycas* frond (top), to the arrangement of the scales in pinecones (center), and to the subtle revolutions atop the baseball plant, *Euphorbia obesa* (bottom).

OPPOSITE: Spiraling scales are on a primitive conifer–a cycad's "fruiting" structures.

PRECEDING PAGE: One frond of blue selection of Mexican fan palm, *Brahea armata*.

Most plants in the mint family (Labiatae or Lamiaceae) have square stems, sets of two leaves opposite each other, and aromatic foliage. This huge family includes the mints, coleus, monarda, *Lamium*, ajuga, hyssop, lavender, *Agastache*, lemon balm, *Nepeta* (the catmints), rosemary, sage, and thyme.

Parsley flowers are borne in clusters with a flat, rounded top; the individual flower stems arising from a single point at the center are called an umbel. Many plants with flowers in this arrangement belong to the carrot family, Umbelliferae, and are called umbellifers. Besides carrot and parsley, there are caraway, celery, dill, fennel, anise, and the weedy wild carrot, Queen Anne's lace. To confuse matters, the umbel form can also be seen in plants that are *not* in the family, such as geraniums, milkweeds like the trailing hoya, and edible and ornamental alliums.

The daisy family is largest of all, with some 1,100 genera and tens of thousands of species and varieties. The scientific name used to be Compositae because many of the cousins' blossoms are composed of showy sterile flowers and insignificant fertile ones. The name has since been changed to Asteraceae as in the huge genus *Aster*.

The sterile flowers form an outer ring of ray florets (what we tend to think of as petals). These florets have evolved to visually attract pollinators to the central floral prize: the cone or, more precisely, disk, of fertile, pollen-bearing flowers. Some family members, however, such as *Achillea* (yarrow), thistles, *Echinops,* and ageratum, have masses of flowers and small or no sterile florets.

The subtle, fertile flowers in the disk are arranged in very specific patterns: an orderly, predictable series of flat curves arcing out from the center. It was these elegant spirals that caught my attention, and the more often I encountered the exquisite configurations in such plants as the single chrysanthemum, *Silphium, Anthemis*, and cosmos, the more I wondered "Why?"

RELATIVE PERFECTION

I suppose one could say I am perennially curious. This desire to learn more about the patterns I'd found in the garden puts me in the august company of men who studied the appearance of sequences and patterns long before me: Pythagoras, the ancient Greek philosopher; Fibonacci, the 13th-century mathematician who introduced the place system of counting to Europe, thereby ending the reign of Roman numerals; and Leonardo da Vinci, the original Renaisance man—scientist, painter, draftsman, engineer, inventor.

What these men have in common is the knowledge of a perfect spatial relationship, what Leonardo called *De divina proportione*, the divine proportion. The relationship compares a section of a line to the whole line, or a square to a rectangle. The ratio is 1 to an approximate number, 1.618. . . .

Pythagoras founded a school in Crotona in southern Italy, where the followers of the order were required to adhere to strict rules of asceticism (Pythagoras

OPPOSITE, CLOCKWISE FROM TOP LEFT: Plant families: Asteraceae, the daisies, is the largest family, with some 24,000 members, including *Rudbeckia laciniata.*

A close-up of yarrow flower head.

A zinnia blossom.

Brassicaceae, the mustard family, include crucifers like broccoflower.

Purple dinosaur kale.

The Rosaceae family includes the rose relative flowering quince (*Chaenomeles*).

Rose cousin *Rubus odorata,* flowering raspberry.

Labiatae, including the nonculinary mountain mint, *Pycnanthemum incana.*

OPPOSITE, CENTER: Berberidaceae, the barberry family, includes the unlikely member *Epimedium.*

invented vegetarianism) and also to seek perfection and harmony in all aspects of life. Their adopted symbol was a pentagram, a five-pointed star within a pentagon, made by drawing lines connecting one corner of the pentagon to another in a prescribed arrangement. The relationship of the length of the side of the pentagon to the length of a line forming the side of the star is always the same: 1 to 1.618.

To my amazement, it was this very same ratio that appeared in the patterns and arrangements I'd discovered in the garden. The seeds in the head of a sunflower, for instance, are arranged in arcs or spirals. There are usually 34 clockwise arcs and 55 counterclockwise arcs. These are called divergent spirals. Sometimes the pairs of numbers are larger: 55 and 89, for instance, or even 89 and 144. But the ratio of spirals in one direction to spirals in the other is always the same: 1 to 1.618.

ABOVE LEFT: The crucifers, or mustard relatives, have four-petaled symmetrical flowers. Many, such as Dame's rocket (*Hesperis matronalis*), are biennial farm weeds.

ABOVE: Members of the parsley family, Umbelliferae (Apiaceae), include carrots, Queen Anne's lace, and, here, *Angelica sylvestris* 'Vicar's Mead'.

flowers of the sun

To 16th-century South American Indians, the sunflower was an earthly symbol of the sun god, the supreme deity above all others. Some of the most prized treasures taken by Francisco Pizarro, the Spanish conquistador who defeated the Inca, were golden sunflower disks worn by Incan priestesses over their breasts.

Sunflowers, introduced by Spanish explorers returning from the Americas, were a hit from the moment the first plant bloomed in European soil. The regal plant soon became prized by royalty, by England's Charles I, for instance, and Louis XIV of France, the "Sun King."

Heli comes from the Greek word for "sun"; *Helios* and versions of this word are

found in the names of several genera. There are scores of plants in the sunflower genus, *Helianthus*. *Helenium autumnale,* sneezeweed plants, produce a generous late-season spectacle when the rest of the garden looks tired. *Helenium* 'Moerheim Beauty' has brick red flowers with mahogany centers, grows 3 to 4 feet tall (and as wide), and will need to be corralled by stakes and string, or a circle of chicken-wire fence, which the vigorous foliage will quickly conceal. 'Butterpat' is a bit shorter and bears a profusion of lemon yellow flowers.

The sunflowers that inspired the Inca and Europeans were the annual *Helianthus annuus*. Many selections and hybrids are easy to grow from seeds and great for children to try, because they sprout fast, shoot up, and flower before kids lose interest. I like the annual strain called 'Italian White', with pale mayonnaise-colored ray flowers and espresso brown disks at the center. The plants produce many flowers on each stem, with successive blooms opening smaller than the first. If you deadhead—that is, cut off the fading flowers as their petals shrivel—the plants will bloom for well over a month. The annual that inevitably gets the most attention is 'Mammoth', which can grow 10 feet tall with a flower head 12 inches across.

Perennial sunflower species, with their bright, cheerful, mostly yellow flowers, still grow wild in the United States. Large stands of *Helianthus maximillianii* (Maximillian sunflower) live in the tall-grass prairie of central Texas. In marshlands of the eastern United States, one might come across *H. angustifolius*, swamp sunflower. Another slender-leaved species is *H. salicifolius*, the willowleaf sunflower. All of these are good garden plants that bloom late in the season, but they tend to flop over in my semishaded garden and must be staked.

DO IT YOURSELF

Nature is often thought to be symmetrical for the most part—for example, two eyes, two ears, etc. But there are asymmetries like the three-petaled lilies and the single blade of grass that sprouts from a seed. The number five also appears in plants like roses. A pentagram—a five-pointed star within a five-cornered pentagon—can be superimposed on top of the five-petaled rose.

1. To discover an amazing fact about the pentagram, start by drawing a pentagon—five equal sides connected at five corners with equal angles.

2. Label the five points of the pentagon clockwise from the top: A, B, C, D, and E.

3. Draw lines connecting the lettered points in this way: A to C; C to E; E to B; B to D; and D to A. You now have a five-pointed star inside the pentagon.

In the middle of the star, you will see a new pentagon where another star could be drawn, and so on, ad infinitum.

The ratio of one of the pentagon sides to any line drawn between the points of the pentagon's corners (that is, the lines forming the interior star) is 1 to approximately 1.618. But that's not all. Examine where each line of the star is intersected (line A–C, for instance, is intersected by line B–E); the ratio of the longer length of line A–C to the entire line's length is, again, 1 to 1.618.

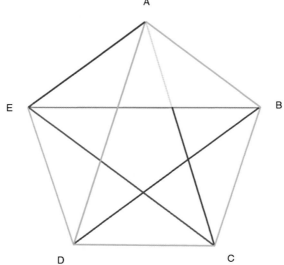

towering pisan

Leonardo Bonacci, an inquisitive mathematician, was the first to document the ratio 1 to 1.618 numerically. Born in about A.D. 1170 in the republic of Pisa, Leonardo traveled with his father, Guilielmo, a diplomat and trade liaison from Pisa, through North Africa, the Middle East, and the southern Mediterranean region. Leonardo was fascinated by the unusual customs and art they encountered, but the boy was particularly interested in the methods different cultures employed for counting and calculations.

Returning to Pisa in 1200, Leonardo began writing about arithmetic, geometry, and algebra. As a youth, he was what we might call a math geek and used the nickname "Bigollo," probably from *bighellone*, meaning "loafer" or "good for nothing." As an adult, he took the name *filius Bonacci,* son of Bonacci, which got shortened to Fibonacci, the name by which he is known today. Fibonacci's observations of Hindu counting and Arabian arithmetic led him to present a critical new concept to the Western world—zero—and instituted the place system in medieval Europe. Thanks to this humble mathematician, we now write "1948" instead of MCMXLVIII. But the discovery to which Fibonacci is most popularly linked is the one that bears his name, the "Fibonacci numbers."

Finding the Fibonacci numbers, or sequence, is simple: beginning with zero and the number one, add the first two numbers to get the subsequent one in the sequence: $0 + 1 = 1$; $1 + 1 = 2$; $1 + 2 = 3$; $2 + 3 = 5$; $3 + 5 = 8$; $5 + 8 = 13$, and so on. So the Fibonacci numbers in this sequence are 0, 1, 1, 2, 3, 5, 8, 13, 21, 34, etc. As you extend the series, the ratio of one number to the next approaches a numerical ratio expressed as 1 to 1.618.

In the case of the sunflower, its spiral of 34 seeds arcing in one direction and 55 in the other, or 55 followed by 89, or 89 followed by 144, are all examples of Fibonacci numbers. And 144 divided by 89 equals 1.6179775. . . .

ABOVE, LEFT TO RIGHT: Spirals appear throughout nature, in seashells; in the unfurling petals of a double rose flower; and in the arrangement of the spiny leaves of *Agave parryi*. The agave's leaves hint at one of evolution's purposes for the spiral in plants—to maximize the light that reaches each leaf.

OPPOSITE: The sunflower exhibits spirals as well, and not for exposure to light and moisture. The reason has to do with a compact arrangement. The sunflower seed head holds seeds in arching rows—some in one direction, and others in opposition. There may be 55 and 89 seeds, or 89 and 144; but the ratio of the number of seeds is always the same—Fibonacci's 1 to 1.618.

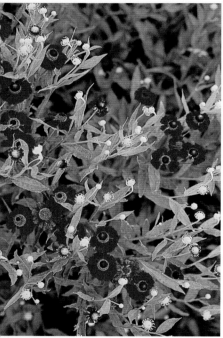

Similarly, when I look at a pinecone, I can see that the scales—the woodlike sections that cover the winged seeds—are arranged in spirals, too. Moisture and cold keep the scales tightly closed, but heat and often fire stimulate them to open wide and allow the seeds to fly away on the wind. Studying the spiral of scales, I found that like the sunflower, some pinecone scales form multiple arcs in one direction while others spiral in the opposite direction. For example, I might count 8 spirals turning counterclockwise and 13 clockwise. There are Fibonacci numbers, again, and the approximate ratio 1 to 1.618.

go for the gold

The patterns found in nature—from the arrangement of seeds in a seed head to the spiral of the Milky Way—may be directives from the universe or they may just be coincidences that mean nothing at all. Regardless of their purpose, effects, or power, their existence is undeniable. You can see the intriguing ratio 1 to 1.618 in seed heads, but how does this relationship have an impact on art?

Centuries before Fibonacci was born, the ratio he documented was already incorporated into art and architecture and even then believed to be the most harmonious geometric relationship of all. When a line is divided in two parts that conform to the ratio, the relationship of the parts is sometimes called the golden section. Taking the ratio one step further, picture a parallelogram that is 1 inch high and 1⅝ inches wide. The shape itself is known as the golden rectangle, and the ratio of the sections is known as the golden mean.

Some people see the golden mean in Mayan architecture, and mathematicians see it in the Great Pyramid of Cheops. The ancient Egyptians are said to have had a "sacred ratio," and this proportion has been referred to in texts as the Egyptian triangle, the triangle of price, and the Kepler triangle, after Johannes Kepler, who in the 1600s wrote "Geometry has two great treasures: one is the theorem of Pythagoras, the other . . . the golden mean." The ancient Greeks applied the proportion to all aspects of art and architecture, including the Parthenon in Athens. The Greeks even applied the ratio to the human body. For instance, it was believed (and recommended as a guide for choosing a wife) that the golden mean defined the perfect proportion in a human body: from toes to navel, and from toes to the top of the head, 1 to 1.618.

LEFT: This sunflower-inspired ceramic box (top) is by artist Ragnar Naess; Helen's flower, *Helenium* 'Moerheim Beauty' (center); variegated *Heliopsis* 'Loraine Sunshine' (bottom).

OPPOSITE: The *Helianthus* genus are the sunflowers, like annual *H. annuus* (left), enduring *H. a.* 'Italian White' (top right), and perennial *H. salicifolia*, the willow-leaf sunflower (bottom right).

Renaissance artists also embraced the golden mean and the golden rectangle. When looking at Leonardo da Vinci's paintings, the fresco *The Last Supper,* or his painting *Annunciation*, for example, one can find many overlapping golden rectangles.

Consciously or not, people find the shape of the golden mean appealing. Modern artists, architects, and designers still apply the golden mean and the golden rectangle in their work; you may witness the alluring ratio anywhere from a 3 × 5 index card to this morning's newspaper.

ALCHEMY

The spirals seen in the sunflower and pinecone as flat curves can also be witnessed in three dimensions, in leaves growing up a stem. Leaves emerge around a stem like the grooves on a screw (screw axis) and at intervals that align to a specific pattern. When I look at a stem from the side, I can see leaves moving up at intervals, much like the steps on a spiral staircase.

Counting down from leaf to leaf until I come to the first leaf that is completely in line with one above leads to a startling revelation. There might be three leaves and five rotations before finding the leaf lying directly below the first one. On another plant, there might be five leaves in eight revolutions. These relationships, the two numbers, can be expressed 3, 5 and 5, 8—Fibonacci numbers once again.

In some plants, such as *Cornus alternifolia,* two leaves emerge from the stem opposite each other. On other plants, coleus and mint, for instance, leaves grow in clusters at each node. Sometimes multiple leaves grow completely around the stem in whorls, as in the martagon lily, whose leaves radiate like spokes of a wheel. Regardless, the angle between the nodes where each leaf or set of leaves emerges conforms to what we might call the golden spiral.

The spiral also shows up in the simple overlapping petals of a single rose, and in the full-blown double rose, with each curved petal partly covered by the next one, all radiating from a central point. Botanists and experts in phyllotaxis —the scientific study of leaf arrangement—concur that the whole of the plant seems to revolve around the spiral, following a pattern revealed in Fibonacci's ratio, the golden mean, and the golden spiral.

UNRAVELING THE SPIRAL

When Leonardo da Vinci observed the golden spiral in leaves around a plant's stem, he surmised correctly that the positioning of leaves allowed as much light, dew, and rainfall as possible to touch every leaf. Plants with leaves that did not shade the ones below, or block dew and rain from hydrating and washing the lower leaves, thrived, prospered, reproduced, and won the contest for natural selection. But this conclusion does not tell the whole story.

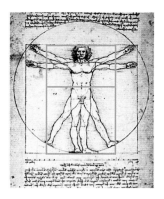

ABOVE: The Roman architect Vitruvius described the perfect human form and Leonardo da Vinci illustrated it in his famous drawing *Vitruvian Man*. Da Vinci did not, however, apply the golden rectangle to the sketch, nor the ancient belief that the perfect human form also corresponds to the golden ratio—the distance from the ground to the navel is 1, and from the ground to the top of the head is 1.618.

OPPOSITE: The flowers of the lily family member *Kniphofia* (vigorous *K.* 'Coral') also display the golden spiral. I planted these below an arch of *Robinia pseudoacacia* 'Lace Lady' ('Twisty Baby'), belonging to the pea family Fabaceae, which is the third largest.

ABOVE, LEFT TO RIGHT: Spirals in the arrangement of leaves can be seen looking down on plants such as hybrid *Daphne* x *burkwoodii* 'Briggs Moonlight'.

The flowers of the ginger *Globba winitii*, dancing ladies, rotate around their dangling stem.

The flower buds and blooms twirl around their stalk on another lily cousin, the fragrant *Hosta plantaginea* 'Grandiflora' (syn. *H. p.* var. *japonica*).

Why is the ubiquitous spiral and ratio of number of leaves so precise? Why do the seed heads of the daisy family exhibit arcs in the same relationship, from purple cornflowers to sunflowers? Because arranging leaves in a spiral up a stalk and packing seeds into a series of spirals is the most efficient allocation of space. Scientific study beyond Leonardo's observations reveals that the spiral facilitates the growth of *meristem* cells—the newest tissue located at the growing points of a plant. The tightly packed cells easily unfurl as they expand. These cells are undifferentiated—like human stem cells—and can grow into various plant parts. As these cells grow and more cells are made, they continue to maintain the spiral as stems elongate, branches spread, and buds open into flowers and produce seeds.

Hostas, members of the lily family, clearly display their spiral flower buds. Aloes and yuccas are lily-family succulents that also show the patterns in leaf and bud. *Kniphofia* species display screw axes in the buds and tubular flowers around their flower spike. You can see the arrangement in the flower buds of the thistles and their gigantic cousins, the cardoon, as well as in the spiral bud we eat, the artichoke.

immortal

When I planned the gravel garden, a walled planting with clay soil and crushed rock for drainage, I decided to defy conventional rules of design. I wanted a collection of disparate plants that I could view up close and admire their individual eccentricities—like the whorls and spirals of the hen-and-chicks clinging to the garden wall.

Collectors' gardens, they say, are hodgepodges of this and that, and a "polka dot" of individual specimens cannot present any semblance of design. The rules, on the other hand, calls for masses of each variety planted so that they flow into

REVEALING THE GOLDEN SPIRAL

Take the Phyllotaxis Challenge: draw plant spirals using golden rectangles.

1. In the center of a piece of paper, draw a horizontal rectangle that measures 5 inches wide by 3 inches tall. This measurement is a fair approximation of the golden rectangle.

2. Next, 3 inches in from the left side of the rectangle, draw a vertical line connecting the top and bottom of the rectangle to form a 3-inch by 3-inch square on the left. Now you have a square and a new, smaller, vertical rectangle to the right. (The ratio of the square compared with the original rectangle is the golden mean.)

3. Draw a line inside the new, vertical rectangle to create a new 2-inch by 2-inch square at the top. This results in a new, horizontal rectangle at the bottom.

4. Next, make a square inside the new horizontal rectangle by drawing a vertical line through it on the left side, which results in a new vertical rectangle on the left. Continue steps 3 and 4 in a clockwise direction until you have seven or eight squares.

Now for the spiral:

1. Beginning at the bottom left corner of the first square, draw an arching line clockwise and upward that touches the top right corner of the square.

2. Allow the arching line to sweep down to the bottom right of this second square.

3. At the corner, continue the arching line into the top right corner of the third square and continue clockwise to the bottom left corner of the third square where it passes into the fourth square at its bottom right.

4. Continue the line clockwise up to the top left corner of the square, into the next square at its bottom left corner, and continue the curve.

Take a look. You have made the spiral that is in the seed head of sunflowers, the arrangement of leaves marching up a plant's stem, and the shell of the chambered nautilus or a snail.

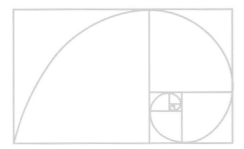

one another. But I wasn't planning a perennial border or an island bed. Instead, I took the advice of my friend Edith Edelman, a garden designer in North Carolina, who shares a passion for growing as many different kinds of plants as she can. In response to the warning about collectors' gardens, she smiles and says she plants in drifts of one and sweeps of two.

I began my drifts and sweeps with the hen-and-chicks and added other succulents and several cacti that have thrived in the gravel garden. There are plenty of sedums that are cold hardy, as well, and the new growth of the tall varieties, which start out looking like little pale green eggs on the ground, clearly exhibit the golden spiral in their overlapping leaves.

Although I have several different varieties of succulents living happily in the gravel garden, the adorable "semps," "hens-and-chicks," or "houseleeks" are particular pets. *Sempervivum* varieties are clearly evergreen and do, in their way, live up to their name: *Semper* = "always," *vivum* = "live" or "live forever." (The curious name "houseleeks" comes from the 14th century when the plants were literally planted to plug the gaps of leaking thatched or turf roofs.) The plants are not truly immortal, of course. In fact they are monocarpic ("one fruit"), which means that after an individual plant flowers, it dies. True annuals and biennials are also monocarps, but the *Sempervivum*, like bromeliads, plan for the future right from the start. By the time a "hen" is mature enough to flower, it is surrounded by a dozen young "chicks" on short or barely apparent stolons (wiry stems), each one of which has the ability to grow, mature, produce chicks of its own, and finally flower.

Unusual, colorful varieties of *Sempervivum* are available from mail-order specialists that publish lists of a hundred or more distinctively different, well-described varieties (but no pictures). It isn't easy to choose plants from written descriptions alone, especially since they all sound so great. While I was searching out my first collection, I could barely believe that these plants would be as different from one another as the catalog promised. I think I bought about 30 from one nursery, and

ABOVE, LEFT TO RIGHT:
In stocky succulents, the spirals of leaves are clear to see, as in *Aeonium* 'Sunburst'.

Silvery *Echeveria* hybrid and *Sedum palmeri*, native to the northeastern slopes of the Sierra Madre Oriental mountains in Mexico, share a pot on the wall overlooking the river.

Tightly packed *Aloe speciosa* flowers may reveal another purpose of the arrangement of buds in plants: to pack as many cells into the smallest space while allowing them to expand, grow, and unfurl.

ABOVE, LEFT TO RIGHT:
Sempervivum ("live forever") look tropical, but are hardy, depending on the variety, to −20°F.

S. arachnoideum hybrids are sometimes called cobweb semps for the silver threads spun from leaf tip to leaf tip.

The common name for *Sempervivum*, hen-and-chicks, refers to the characteristic of growing babies around the adult. These plants are monocarpic: they mature, bloom, bear seed, and die; by then the chicks are ready to take their parent's place.

when they arrived, I was surprised to see that no two were alike. One had gold leaves, another was copper-colored. There was a particularly interesting plant with cylindrical green leaves that have black coloring on the blunt, stubby tips, which appear to have been snipped off.

I was also drawn to the "spider-web" species and varieties, such as *S. arachnoideum,* small plants covered with "spun" white threads from leaf tip to leaf tip. *S. soboliferum,* another favorite, grows into mossy carpets of tiny globular rosettes that often produce rootless chicks hanging on to their parent's slender stolons. These chicks drop to the ground, root, and form their own evergreen colony.

When we think of evergreens, we usually picture conical conifers with needle leaves like Christmas trees. But the southern magnolia is a broad-leaved evergreen, as are rhododendrons and hardy *Yucca filamentosa,* a species in a genus of mostly tender plants. The hardy yucca is not an herbaceous perennial that dies to the ground in winter but a semiwoody, semisucculent shrub or subshrub. What looks like a bunch of wide blades of grass has a stem down inside, and in time the stem will grow taller, giving it an appearance much like a palm tree.

The typical hardy yucca is called Adam's needle for the flower stem that rises 2 feet or more above the 2-foot-tall swordlike foliage; 1-inch-wide, waxy white, outfacing bells grow from the "needle." But the species is a victim of contempt bred by familiarity. Like many other plants that require very little care, the hardy yucca is taken for granted by most of us, relegated to gas-station corner plantings and parking lots. Despite its indestructibility, I too find it hard to get excited about the plain graygreen species.

However, there are several eye-catching variegated evergreen yuccas that will bring a hard-edged, "architectural" element to landscape plantings. *Y. filamentosa* 'Variegata' is a popular variation, with gray-green leaves edged in white. 'Bright Edge' has green leaves edged in vivid yellow margins. 'Gold Heart' offers green leaves with canary yellow centers. The rich green leaves on 'Golden Sword' are

ABOVE, LEFT TO RIGHT: The hedgehog agave (*A. stricta*) is a succulent (hardy to 15°F) that forms a hemisphere of narrow, spiky leaves.

Yuccas are sub-shrubs, similar to agaves. The dull green species *Y. filamentosa* becomes spectacular in the variegated forms, such as *Y. f.* 'Golden Sword'– yellow with green margins, and the reverse *Y. f.* 'Bright Edge'.

Some of the yuccas are quite cold-hardy, easily withstanding temperatures below 0°F. They add a unique look to the winter garden, but by the season's end, after snowfalls and frigid winds, the plants may be tattered. Cut the leaves back to the woody central stalk, and in no time, fresh, colorful swords will take their place.

OPPOSITE: *Sempervivum* hybrids grow in the crevices of the top of the wall of my gravel garden, where they bake in the heat of summer and enjoy excellent drainage.

marked by vibrant lemon yellow stripes in the center and make the striking plant welcome in the winter landscape as its leaves pierce through the snow cover.

Young plants (propagated from pups—side growths removed and rooted) grow into globes of spiky foliage. Unlike some other varieties (for me, at least), 'Golden Sword' doesn't get as tattered by harsh weather until the very end of winter. Cutting off the old leaves completely has a shocking result at first, but lush new growth quickly fills the void.

When the leaves are cut off, the yucca's short trunk very much resembles a pineapple fruit. The old leaves grew in a spiral, and the new ones will, as well. Even the flowers spiral up the flower spike.

It is easy to believe there is divinity in nature when I look at the elaborate, eloquent, and regimented pattern of yucca leaves and flowers, as well as the leaves of other plants, seeds in a fruit, branches, and even branching roots that conform to the divine proportion and reveal the golden mean.

No one knows if Fibonacci ever related his ratio to plants, or studied plants at all. I wonder if he would have been surprised to find his numerical discoveries exhibited so clearly in nature. I suspect not. My guess is that he would have instead expected and accepted the remarkable.

ARTS & FLOWERS

I planned the garden in New Jersey, in part, to be an outdoor studio where I could grow plants and create garden schemes to write about and photograph. I imagined I could be there when the light was perfect, when every plant was at its peak. I could shoot on overcast days (the best), early in the morning (in my bathrobe!), or during the hour of twilight while dinner was on the grill. I have an ongoing fantasy (as yet to be realized) of never having to leave.

When I went to art school, we students had a phrase, "making art," fit for every occasion. ("Can't help you move the piano; got to go make art.") I still feel the need to make art, create, and share. Today, I'm busy with writing, photographing, lecturing, and broadcasting, but I have to admit that I feel happiest working in 3-D (sculpting in earth, clay, concrete) and 4-D (gardening). When the medium is living plants, the fourth dimension is time.

Growing up, my heroes were artists such as the sculptor Augustus St. Gaudens, whose public works include entrances to New York's Central Park. My own great-uncle Victor David Brenner sculpted the bas-relief of President Lincoln that still graces our penny. I felt a connection to such painters as Edward Burne-Jones, who created romantic allegories, and to illustrators such as Aubrey Beardsley, who drew idiosyncratic pen-and-ink drawings that were spicy enough to excite any duplicitous Victorian. Alphonse Mucha practically invented the poster as art, and Maxfield Parrish, illustrator of storybook fantasies, also painted spectacular landscapes for Edith Wharton's book *Italian Villas and Their Gardens.*

Nineteenth-century landscape architects also made art. Andrew Jackson Downing influenced a half-century of American house-and-garden architecture, and his friend Frederick Law Olmsted designed Central Park in New York City and other municipal works around the country. These men and their supporters felt that a connection to nature was a human necessity, and they recognized the place of art and of plants in landscape architecture. I felt particular kinships with Norwegian-born Jens Jensen, who championed

the use of local native plants in his American Midwest gardens, and Irishman William Robinson, who "invented" and popularized the naturalistic garden style in England 150 years ago. He wrote, "The rightness of plants allowed their natural settings."

Robinson's era attracted me because it was a time when plants inspired artists: garden designers, skilled painters, illustrators, writers, and even composers who honored and glorified botanical forms. These people sought to bring nature and beauty into everyone's life (and so do I).

GARDEN ART

No one is certain when living plants were first used as decoration, although they have been the subjects of art for millennia. Some 10,000 years ago, at the beginning of the Neolithic Period, or the New Stone Age, humans began to form larger groups, create communities, and farm. They recorded everyday details of their lives on cave walls—a visual journal of sorts. Later, drawings of edible and medicinal plants, as well as those used for religious and mystical purposes, were scratched into wet clay pottery. Plants soon found their way into ornament and personal adornment as well; depictions of acanthus leaves graced the capitals of the Romans' Corinthian columns, for instance, and jewelry bearing images of plants and birds and even a pomegranate pendant in faience glass have been discovered in Egypt.

Painted frescoes and mosaics from Pompeii showing living plants grown in containers and cut flowers placed in vases are among the earliest depictions of plants grown for decoration. Illustrations of newly found plants were commissioned by

botanists, but these drawings and watercolor paintings intended for scientific study also fueled the imagination of artists, and soon the latest discoveries were immortalized in the still lifes of the old Dutch masters and French painters. The Empress Josephine, the first wife of Napoleon I, commissioned the Flemish-born painter Pierre Joseph Redouté to preserve and commemorate her roses in the garden at Malmaison.

In the second half of the 19th century, artists felt that beauty and nature were the most important things to have in life, that plants represented both, and that flowers could and should decorate everything from needlepoint to soap boxes. The designer William Morris wrote, "Have nothing in your houses that you do not know to be useful, or believe to be beautiful."

Morris planted gardens at Red House in suburban London and filled them with flowers he loved, including columbine, yellow iris, dog rose, and common primrose. These plants and many other favorites found their way into his wallpaper and fabric schemes, and even inspired the poetry he wrote.

The American impressionist painter Childe Hassam immortalized Celia Thaxter's island garden in New Hampshire. Claude Monet planted entire gardens in Giverny, France, to capture on canvas; his famous representations of his verdigris green bridge festooned with wisteria and his huge painted water-lily tableaus are only a few of many examples of the artwork his garden inspired.

The American artist John Singer Sargent was so keen on portraying the quality of twilight in the garden, he spent two autumns (1885 and 1886) painting in the last few minutes before the sun dipped below the horizon for his masterpiece *Carnation, Lily, Lily, Rose*. The painting depicts two young girls lighting lanterns while standing among white lilies that have been rendered larger than life-size to give the impression of a child's view of the garden.

ABOVE, LEFT TO RIGHT:
The artist Maxfield Parrish, known best for his fantasy fairytale paintings, illustrated Edith Wharton's 1904 book, *Italian Villas and Their Gardens*.

John Singer Sargent spent two autumns painting in the last minutes before the sun dipped below the horizon to capture the special light for his painting *Carnation, Lily, Lily, Rose*. He exaggerated the angle and the size of the flowers to amplify a child's perspective of the garden.

Villa Gamberaia was painted by Maxfield Parrish in 1903.

good taste

Oscar Wilde, whose personal emblem was the lily, proclaimed that he and his fellow writers and artists—idealists like William Morris—were dedicated to "art for art's sake." These men championed the Aesthetic Movement in England, which took its name from the Greek *aisthētikos,* meaning perception of good taste and the science of beauty. The movement blossomed as a backlash against the Industrial Revolution, decrying not only the bad design churned out by machines and their masters but also the harmful impact mass production had on society.

The Aesthetes proposed that there be affordable products for all people. Instead of the pedestrian manufactured goods, which they called "philistine," or the heavy ornamentation of high Victorian design, these early minimalists recommended that every utensil, swath of fabric, roll of wallpaper, piece of furniture—in other words, all goods and even the packages they came in—should be tastefully and beautifully designed.

Gardens for pleasure, until the era of the Aesthetes in the mid-19th century, were the privilege of only the very rich. The emerging middle class made possible by the Industrial Revolution wanted gardens of their very own and adopted the design that dominated their wealthier counterparts' gardens: carpet bedding—rigid beds of annuals in parterre plantings. The Aesthetes railed against carpet bedding, promoting instead the informality of nature embodied in the woodlands of Britain. Richard Mabey, the English nature writer, criticized formal bedding in his introduction to the 1983 edition of William Robinson's book *The Wild Garden* (originally published in 1870): "Tender and often rather garish flowers from Imperial outposts were laboriously raised in greenhouses, planted out in dead straight rows and symmetrical formations (with the exact spaces between each plant kept quite bare for contrast), allowed their brief season of brilliance and then ripped out again. Gardeners were not so much plant stewards as drill sergeants."

Robinson's original book triggered a quiet revolution calling for naturalistic garden design. This approach, and the development of the herbaceous border (inspired by the humble cottage gardens chronicled in Robinson's 1883 best seller, *The English Flower Garden*), set forth the guiding principles of the Arts and Crafts garden, a style that spread through Great Britain to the United States, and continues to influence design today.

OPPOSITE, CLOCKWISE FROM TOP: The Aesthetes believed that art should be available to everyone and appear in everyday objects, such as this detail of an American tin can label with an asymmetrical, Japonesque influence.

Mohonk Mountain House in New Paltz, New York, maintains the tradition of bedding out annuals in patterned plantings.

In his popular book *The English Flower Garden*, reknowned British garden writer William Robinson recommended colorful, naturalistic plantings.

Robinson advocated an egalitarian antidote to rigid bedding, instead looking to nature for inspiration as might be imagined in this modern interpretation with naturalized daffodils.

Victorian plantings were symmetrical with formality from mirrored elements, like the planted urns at Merriam House in Newton, New Jersey.

the brotherhood

I can identify with the activist-artists working in England in the second half of the 19th century. They promoted quality and equality, art and socialism—better working conditions, beauty in every person's life, and egalitarian gardening for pleasure and the enrichment of the soul. And they considered nature divine.

The English art critic John Ruskin wrote:

"Go to Nature in all singleness of heart, and walk with her laboriously and trustingly, having no other thoughts but how best to penetrate her meaning, rejecting nothing, selecting nothing, and scorning nothing; believing all things to be right and good, and rejoicing always in the truth."

In 1848, English art-school students Dante Gabriel Rossetti, John Everett Millais, and William Holman Hunt founded the Pre-Raphaelite Brotherhood, or the PRB. These men shared a rebellious spirit, ecclesiastical reverence, and youth (Hunt was 10 years old when he first entered the Royal Academy of Art). The brotherhood's name refers to early Renaissance art up to the time (1483–1520) of the boy-genius Raphael (Raffaello) Sanzio. Raphael's early paintings were devotional and conservative. (When he was 20, he painted a nativity scene with a fully clothed baby Jesus.) But the PRB considered the artists of the following decades, the self-proclaimed "Mannerists," decadent, even vulgar. These works featured muddy colors and an emphasis on style over substance in their exaggerated perspective and stylized elongated figures. (One well-known Mannerist painting is actually titled *Madonna with Long Neck*.)

The PRB students protested against the state of art and art instruction at the Royal Academy of Art, and in particular the influence of Sir Joshua Reynolds, the founder of the academy, whom they called "Sir Sloshua" for what they saw as his sloppy painting, artifice, and rigid adherence to the rules of Mannerism. The PRB sought truth in art, to paint things that were real—plants and flowers as they grew in meadows, or a birch copse carpeted by wild daffodils—not depictions of pantheist myths or pink cherubs. The men wanted to return to "religious and cultural archaism," the "clean line" and "simple faith" of the Quattrocento (15th-century Italian art), the rich detail and intense colors of the Medieval Byzantine mosaics and illuminated manuscripts.

Although the young revolutionaries felt that they were leading the art world into the future, their contributions were somewhat parochial and their works had a repressive formality. The portraits they produced were flat and often in profile (the profile feels voyeuristic rather than inclusive), throwbacks to paintings created before the "discovery" of perspective. Despite everyday settings and ostensibly humble dress, the PRB subjects—heroic figures from religion and literature—were usually clothed in rich forest green and vivid russet velvet. Although these neocon artists promoted Christian values, they also believed in free expression. Rossetti's

ABOVE: One of the three founders of the Pre-Raphaelite Brotherhood, Dante Gabriel Rossetti depicted strong, red-haired women in romantic works, such as *Venus Verticordia,* painted between 1864–68, with flowers like roses and honeysuckle.

OPPOSITE: Henriette Suhr's garden Rocky Hills in Mount Kisco, New York, captures the romance and relaxed naturalism of the post-Victorian garden style, reinterpreted in the late 20th century as the Natural Garden.

TOP: The passionflower is named as a symbol of the passion of Christ, with petals for the ten faithful apostles; corona for the crown of thorns; stamens for the five wounds; and the stigmas for the nails.

ABOVE: *Lilium longiflorum* (Easter lily) and *L. candidum* were symbols of purity in paintings.

poems and paintings, for instance, had an erotic lushness. He was known to have had affairs with many of the women he painted, including Jane Morris, married at the time to the designer William Morris.

These three "free thinkers" made a tremendous impact on art and society, despite the fact that the PRB disbanded just three years after it was formed. Their work would inspire artists for the rest of the century, and infuse painting, literature, and even garden design with romantic naturalism.

pious passion

One of my favorite paintings is John Everett Millais's portrayal of *Hamlet*'s Ophelia. It was unusual for the PRB to portray a character from Shakespeare, preferring instead the Arthurian legends, but in 1852 Millais rendered a recently deceased Ophelia floating face up in a decidedly organic pool. The fully clothed Ophelia, eyes open, lies in water strewn with spring garden flowers such as daffodils, forget-me-nots, and English bluebells, along with a rose that has dropped its petals onto the water. The background was painted during the summer of 1851 on the River Ewell in Surrey, and the human model, a very much alive 19-year-old named Elizabeth Siddal, posed repeatedly over several months that following winter—in a bathtub with water heated by lamps from below. One day, the lamps went out and the temperature of the water dropped dramatically, but Siddal did not complain. She did, however, suffer from ill health for much of her life. (Siddal later married Rossetti, but she died from an overdose of the poppy derivative laudanum at the age of 33.)

The devotion to craft had no limits, and neither did the art of devotion. Flowers often appeared in paintings with spiritual subtexts, such as PRB follower Charles Allston Collins's most famous work, *Convent Thoughts* (1851)—which depicts a nun in a garden. She stands between two flower beds by the edge of a tiny pool inhabited by water lilies and goldfish. The flowers in the garden include gladioli, martagon lilies, a few small double roses, blue sage, fuchsia, agapanthus, and Madonna lilies (*Lilium candidum*), the holy flower of Mary. *L. candidum* was often included in Annunciation paintings of the Middle Ages and early Renaissance. *Candidum* means "white," but the lily was said to have been yellow until Mary touched it.

At the time *Convent Thoughts* was painted, it was attacked in England for its religious piety, or worse: the men of the Pre-Raphaelite Brotherhood were frequently accused of being Roman Catholic sympathizers. The nun holds a prayer book in her left hand, but the subject of her intense focus is in her right hand, a blossom that appears in many paintings and decorative arts: *Passiflora*, the passionflower.

People today may imagine that the "passion" derives from the possible effects of eating the fruit or drinking its juice. But the name of the plant has a different meaning. Sixteenth-century Jesuit missionaries first came upon the passionflower in South America when they arrived with the conquistadores. One legend claims

SAY IT WITH FLOWERS

The "meaning" of a plant may be seen in its common name, such as forget-me-nots or the weeping willow associated with mourning. It isn't difficult to guess that a red rose sends love, or the white lily means purity. Oaks have been associated with hospitality, strength, tenacity, and stability, and the acorn was a symbol of life renewed. Some sources claim that the Victorians frequently communicated via flowers and bouquets. Other references disagree, suggesting that the meanings were not set but were more the arbitrary invention of poets.

Kate Greenaway, a well-known 19th-century artist, wrote and illustrated popular children's books during her career. In the 1880s she published *Language of Flowers,* recording for anyone who needed it a flower-to-English and English-to-flower dictionary.

Imagine young Victorian courting: The couple would not be allowed to meet without a chaperone. She could not address him by his first name, and he could certainly not profess his ardor in spoken word; but he might send flowers. An almond flower would speak of his hope; an apricot blossom, his timid love. A single gardenia would say "I love you in secret." A mallow would speak of gentle affection, while a magnolia blossom would tell her that he saw her as sweet and beautiful. A fuchsia also confided his love, and the amaranth declared that his love would never fade.

She might respond with an unfortunate sign of ambiguity: acacia blossoms signifying only friendship, platonic love at best. Moss said charity and nothing more. Meadow saffron stated, point blank, that their would-be relationship was over. He might respond to such a rebuff with a gift of nuts, which translates today exactly as it did then—"You are crazy!"

If she reconsidered, she might recant her rejection with a lotus leaf. He might express remorse for his rebuke with raspberries, swear that he would be hers until death with a yucca, or perhaps even propose with phlox.

When picking flowers as a gift from the garden, one could consider meanings published in various Victorian sources, or invent your own. A length of ivy vine could symbolize the continuity of friendship, and flower buds, hope for the future.

ABOVE: A *Magnolia* x *soulangiana* selection says "sweet and beautiful."

ABOVE, LEFT TO RIGHT:
Passiflora manicata is a popular and floriferous, if a little too vigorous, passion-flower vine in California gardens.

Among the easiest water plants to bring into flower are the day-blooming blue tropical water lilies. Plants can be overwintered in a cool dark place, and need not be soaking wet.

Victoria water lily flowers open white, and turn pink after pollination. The pads grow up to 6 feet across.

OPPOSITE: Sir Joseph Paxton was the first to bring the *Victoria* into bloom, and for this he was knighted. The underside of each giant pad has a thorny network of buttresses up to 4 inches tall. Paxton incorporated the structure into his designs for the Crystal Palace.

that in his visions, Saint Francis saw a vine growing on the cross. The Jesuits believed the *Passiflora* to be that vine, and named it *Flor de las cionco llagas*, flower of the five wounds, or *Flor passionis*. To them, the symbolism was obvious: the ten outer petals represented the ten faithful apostles—Judas excluded for his betrayal, and Peter because he deceived Jesus. The corona is the crown of thorns. Five stamens symbolize the five wounds. The ovary, the hammer, and the three stigmas—the top of the female organ—are the three nails. In other interpretations, the stigma stands for the Holy Trinity. When the missionaries observed the indigenous people eating the fruit, they took it to mean the natives hungered for Christianity.

GLASS LILY

After the Napoleonic Wars, Britain had no rival in the world. Railroads, optimism, and the focus on science and industry converged, turning the country into a massive machine. The success of textile manufacturing and innovations in iron fabrication brought great wealth to capitalists. Mass production increased the quantity of products available to all people, even of modest means, but as the PRB artist-reformers were lamenting, the quality and especially the design were poor. Queen Victoria's husband, Prince Albert, decided something had to be done to address the situation.

Seeing the success of the French during the Industrial Exhibition of 1844, German-born Prince Albert resolved to celebrate his adopted country's achievements in a similar venue, with a world's fair: The Great Exhibition of the Works of Industry of All Nations of 1851. His plan was to inspire England's manufacturers to step up to the challenge for this fabulous event and improve both the quality and the appearance of their products.

The idea called for a temporary hall, much larger than that of the French exhibition, budgeted at £230,000. The building would occupy the grounds of Hyde Park in London for an entire year. More than 230 architects competed for the com-

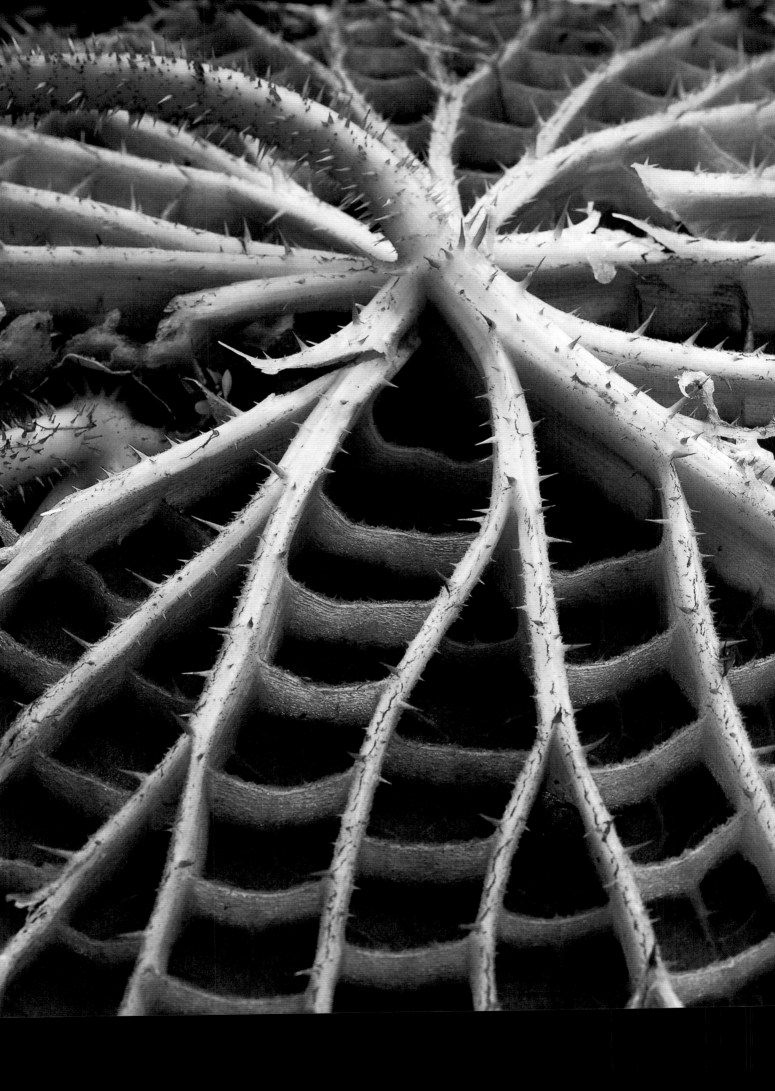

Colors were artfully arranged and harmonized in Jekyll gardens, and although her work has come to be synonymous with the "English garden," featuring pale blues, mauve, and lavender-pinks, she was just as likely to make red-hot borders with flaming oranges, pale and vivid yellows, and deep crimson flowers.

Jekyll's gardens were famous during her lifetime and well known from her writings, and from articles by other authors, since writers, artists, horticulturists, and garden designers from around the world would make pilgrimages to Munstead Wood to see Miss Jekyll's "perfect pictures." Jekyll had become an artist after all; she combined formal architecture and design with deceptively casual tousles of flowers to create living masterpieces.

JAPONISM

Eleven years after the opening of the Great Exhibition of 1851, the International Exhibition of 1862 featured a Morris and Company display that was praised for the exactness of its representation of the Middle Ages. But medievalists would soon be taken by something completely new to them, something that would ignite a craze in England and Europe. The feudal system in Japan was ending, the days of the shoguns had come to an end, and after 250 years of isolation, there was a consensus that it was better to join the Western powers, in particular Great Britain, than to be beaten by them. The British had been interested in Japan for centuries, and the Americans wanted Japan as a refueling stop for their new steam-powered navy. The Japanese decided to expose their world to the rest of the planet, using the 1862 London exhibition to do so.

Until that time, most Japanese artwork was known mainly from the paper wrapped around exported goods. Visitors to the exposition were stunned but smitten with the Japanese exhibits, and artists were inspired by what they saw: ink drawings and calligraphy; painted flowers decorating screens; peonies, tree peonies, and cherry blossoms rendered in pale colors and with Oriental simplicity. Western designers drank it all in.

The asymmetry prevalent in Japanese artistry was truly revolutionary to the Aesthetes. Imagine what it might have been like to see for the first time a chest or cabinet without mirror-image doors; the concept was a shock to the Western sensibility.

Japan's entries at the exhibition started a fad in the United Kingdom. Soon nearly every English household displayed a Japanese fan on the mantelpiece. Arthur Lasenby Liberty opened a shop, Liberty & Co., in London in 1875, selling ornaments, fabrics, and art objects from Japan. Gilbert and Sullivan were inspired to capitalize on the popularity with a comic opera, their enormously successful, invented interpretation of Japanese life: *The Mikado*.

Many of the Aesthetic Movement designers fell under the spell of Japonism, including Christopher Dresser, a man whose often quoted remark "Knowledge is

TOP: The exotic Japanese tree peony impressed foreign visitors in 1862.

ABOVE: An herbaceous peony and *Spirea thunbergii* in a Japanese-inspired vase featuring lotus leaves and imagined blue flowers.

OPPOSITE: The opening of the borders of Japan in 1862 flooded the design and garden world with plants like flowering cherry trees.

power" is better known today than his name or his work. Dresser was a highly respected industrial designer, botanist, botanical illustrator, and teacher in his day. Influenced by Asian art, he adopted the Anglo-Japanese style of angular motifs and asymmetry in his designs for indoor and outdoor furniture, silver, and pottery commissiond by such companies as Minton and Wedgwood.

His sophisticated, efficient creations refined the populist notions of the Aesthetic Movement: these works *could* be found in an average middle-class person's home. But in a short time, these spare designs would be passé. Simplicity was about to give way to ornamentation, not in the heavy Victorian manner but in an anti-English notion of design that was new, free, and playful—perfect for the pleasure-seeking generation of the Belle Epoch and its Art Nouveau.

NEW ART

The name Art Nouveau was secured in the public's consciousness when, in 1895, Japanese-art collector Siegfried Bing opened his new gallery in Paris: La Maison de l'Art Nouveau (The House of the New Art). The new art, with organic shapes and motifs from nature, swept turn-of-the-century Europe. The industrial designer, architect, and sculptor Hector Guimard fashioned streetlights in the shape of sprouting trees for the Paris Metro stations, with vine tendrils weaving through iron balustrades. In Spain, Antonio Gaudí produced unique, "sculpted" buildings made of twisted steel covered with concrete and studded with tile and glass. In the 1890s, Belgian master architect Victor Horta designed interiors with botanical interpretations painted on walls, in tiled floors, and cast on balustrades and lighting. Art Nouveau interior decor, decorative accessories, and household goods flourished in Prague, Budapest, and Krakow, the center of *Mloda Polska*, the new Poland Movement.

The Scottish painter Margaret Macdonald exhibited at the first Vienna Secession Exhibition in 1897, a show that highlighted works of the *Jugendstil* (youth style), the German version of Art Nouveau. The building designed by architect Joseph Maria Olbrich to hold the second Vienna Secession Exhibition, in 1898, epitomized the Germanic and modernized version of florid Art Nouveau. This exhibition featured furniture and decorative objects by the brilliant designer Josef Hoffmann, whose work is as fresh today as it was a hundred years ago. The semiabstract portraits of bejeweled men and women against backgrounds of liquid gold by Austrian Gustav Klimt were also shown that year, and it seems Klimt may have been influenced by Margaret Macdonald's work shown the previous year.

LEFT: An iron panel in the style of Charles Eastlake exhibits Japanese influence (top); a painting of checkered lily, *Fritillaria meleagris*, by architect Charles Rennie Mackintosh (center); Victor Horta incorporated botanical flourishes into iron work and decoration for his Art Nouveau architecture (bottom).

SOMETHING TO LEAN ON

In the garden, we can use vines to create living art; trellises, arbors, arches, and pergolas swathed in green are a welcome addition to any garden. I like to grow vines where I can keep an eye on them. Many have a tendency to grow a little too well and can get out of hand if not watched, pruned, and otherwise coaxed into submission. For me, an ideal spot was on the exterior of the sunroom.

I covered the outside walls with trelliswork made of white-dyed recycled plastic so I would not have to paint it. The plastic is weaker than wood, so I affixed it with brackets made of hollow plastic, and reinforced it with wooden 2x4s slipped inside.

I pruned all but two vertical shoots of the sinewy wisteria to the ground when it was young in order to discourage such a strong-arm vine from growing between the house and the trellis, which might bend or twist the plastic frame. I supported the two vertical shoots by loosely tying them to the trellis until they reached the brackets at the top of the porch, where I allowed them to spread horizontally.

It's not the blooms alone that fascinate me with vining plants like wisteria. It's the different ways they climb. The climbing gloriosa lily, for instance, has leaf tips that twist around other plants' stems. Clematis leaf petioles (leaf stems) gently wrap around supports, which makes this vine a perfect partner for a trellis, or a rose for that matter. Specialized petioles on many vines have evolved into tendrils: grapevines have tendrils that are soft and green when they are growing and then turn stiff and woody, while those of sweet peas and cup-and-saucer vine (*Cobaea scandens*) are slender, curly, and almost sticky. Passion-flower vines have tendrils as well, and when they *feel* something they can grow around, they grab it and then coil, tightening their spirals to bring the main stems closer to the support. The idea of a plant "feeling" is not inaccurate. A young growing shoot of a vine such as a pole bean, morning glory, or a honeysuckle will swing in arcs as it grows, drawing

CONTINUED...

ABOVE: My sun porch embellished with recycled plastic trellis for vines.

circles in the air, hunting for a suitable support. When the shoot touches something, cells on one side of the stem grow at an accelerated rate, which causes the vine to wind. This natural spiraling is almost impossible to replicate: when I try to wrap an errant stem around a support, it will usually unwrap itself. Worse still, winding a stem the "wrong way"—Chinese wisteria (*Wisteria sinensis*) winds clockwise, while Japanese wisteria (*W. floribunda*) winds counterclockwise, for example—can actually set back the growth of the plant.

Other climbing plants have barbs or hooks that help them grab, like the thorns of a rose. Climbing hydrangea (*Hydrangea anomala* subsp. *petiolaris)* and *Schizophragma* species use short, hairlike rootlets. *Parthenocissus* species and varieties have "holdfasts," growths about ½ inch long that end in flat disks at the tips and have a natural glue to secure them to trees or buildings, a bit like a tree frog's toes. The weight of some of the more vigorous plants—ivy, for instance—can be too much for tree limbs and should be removed, which can be as simple as cutting the plant at the ground, killing the top growth. Short rootlets can damage mortar in buildings and walls when the freeze-thaw cycle expands the plant tissues; such movement can pulverize concrete, brick, or mortar.

How can I reconcile my feelings for nature and still grow a plant that I see as, well, potentially dangerous? The gardener in me wrestles constantly with the environmentalist; the agronomist argues with the ecologist. It is nearly impossible to justify or rationalize away my dilemma. If the vine is a local species, one that is indigenous to the area, such as

ABOVE, FROM LEFT: The sculptural stems of wisteria. An early-20th-century iron gate at Greenwood Gardens, Short Hills, New Jersey, is by Samuel Yellin.

ABOVE, LEFT TO RIGHT:
The first iris to appear in late winter is bulbous *I. reticulata*. Miniature dwarf bearded iris bloom next followed by dwarf bearded. Dwarf bearded iris 'Pilgrims' Choice' is from 1990.

Japanese iris (*I. enstata*) and yellow flag (*I. pseudacorus*)—a late-flowering iris with leaves softly striped pale yellow and light green. Large, lemon yellow flowers bloom for nearly a month since the plant is a mule, sterile. Instead of putting its energy into setting seed, the plant continues to flower—trying in vain to set seed.

I am also growing more "remontant," or reblooming, irises that flower again in late summer to extend the season into fall. The short-in-stature white-flowered bearded iris called 'Frequent Flyer' is the last iris to bloom in my garden. I suppose the only thing better than an eye-grabbing plant that stops the show is one that is able to do an encore.

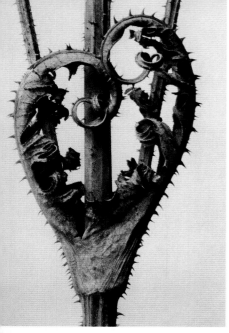

UP CLOSE AND PERSONAL

I am a collector, and there are a few drawbacks to this passion (disorder, some might say). Not only do I want to try every plant I can, I do. "So many plants, so little space."

Of course, I love propagating and sharing plants, especially if they are rare or local natives, or easy to divide, like the bearded iris. If I lose one, I may be able to get a piece back from someone to whom I've given a plant.

One way I can collect a plant, even if I do not grow it, is to capture its soul—record its stunning beauty in a photograph. A daylily flower lasts but a single day, but its image lives on (even if the plant does not). On overcast days, camera on tripod, I create portraits of individual plants, buds, blooms, leaves, and seedpods. Among my goals in photographing and writing about plants is to show and tell people about things they have never seen before, or simply overlooked.

Many years ago, I came across the 19th-century photographs of Karl Blossfeldt. A remarkable geometry appeared in his extreme close-ups. Here was someone who had spent his life doing what I was hoping to do—show people that the most remarkable things might be right before their eyes, standing ready to inspire.

Blossfeldt started his career as a botanical model-maker. He was also a teacher, industrial designer, wrought-iron monger, and sculptor. He added photographer to his credits when he began taking photographs—glass slides—for students in his class, "Modeling from Plants," at the School of Art and Design in Berlin-Charlottenburg. His photos supported his premise that the best engineering, textile, and industrial designs had already been anticipated in nature. This self-taught photographer thought of his images as teaching aids, and left very few notes on his methods.

Blossfeldt might have drifted into obscurity if he had not been "discovered" by Karl Nierendorf, a banker and collector versed in Dada and Constructivism. Prints of Blossfeldt's slides were made using the photogravure process popular from the late 1800s through the first half of the 20th century. An exhibition was mounted in 1928 with Nierendorf's help, and Blossfeldt published his first book, *Urformen der Kunst* (*Art Forms in Nature*), which was followed by another, *Wundergarten in der Natur* (*Magic Garden of Nature*), in 1932, the year Karl Blossfeldt died. More than 60 years later, Americans discovered Blossfeldt's prints and started framing reproductions of his graphic images to hang on their walls.

My photographs don't look like Blossfeldt's, but I hope to engage and inspire in similar ways, showing people the natural beauty that surrounds them every day.

LEFT: Karl Blossfeldt looked to plants for inspiration and showed students glass slides of teasel (top) and curly leaves (center). Examples in industrial design (bottom).

OPPOSITE: I find inspiration in plants like cup-and-saucer vine (*Cobaea scandens*).

PART FOUR

growing forward

Gardens, like the gardeners who nurture them, change with time. Vines climb skyward through the years. Trees, the most venerable of plants, travel through the cycles of their lives, and many will be here after we are gone. Gardens move (like my plants from the container garden in SoHo, to the brownstone backyard in Brooklyn, and some to New Jersey). Planting beds become filled with roots; shade appears where there once was sunlight. As I get older, I find that I am focusing more on less—individual prized plants close to the house, for instance. And I've come to rely on and find a new appreciation for, self-sufficient varieties chosen to grow beside the paths walked less often.

OPPOSITE: Rose of Sharon, *Hibiscus syriacus* 'Diana', blooms longest since it rarely makes fruit.

HOMEGROWN DISCOVERIES

My relationship with plants began as a simple matter of love at first sight: I came, I saw, they conquered. Now, after a lifetime of gardening, I recognize that a successful perennial border, with plants that pick up the slack in down times, has to be a mixed border. This means plenty of woody plants and shrubs, especially those with colorful or textural leaves and pleasing shapes.

The search for these plants led me back to old-fashioned favorites: plants such as hydrangea, viburnum, and deutzia, species that had stood the test of time and had rewarded gardeners for decades before me. Many of these plants have been overlooked, forgotten, or replaced by fashionable, "new and improved" versions, but I liked that the old standards were easy to propagate and could be shared with friends who had all sorts of gardening situations.

As I started to gather these old-fashioned charmers, I discovered that they had an added bonus I hadn't anticipated: these plants were remarkably self-reliant. They required minimal investment of time for spectacular returns in blooms, structure, and seasonal foliage. Lowering maintenance wasn't really my goal, but it has become a wonderful by-product of using self-sufficient plants, ones I've come to think of as "stalwarts." A plant that tastes bad won't get eaten, for instance; one that has water-retaining capacities sails through times of drought; others suppress weeds by competing with them for water and shading the soil beneath their leaves. In essence the stalwarts get by with little attention from me.

Of course, the stalwarts in my garden may not behave similarly in your garden. To find your own independent varieties, I suggest that you do what I do: look for local plants first, then investigate some old-fashioned favorites. Cemeteries are often a good place to find shrubs, as the ones growing there are doing well with little or no care. To find old-fashioned plants that perform well in your particular situation, it's also helpful to check old photographs of houses and gardens in your area.

My search for stalwarts led me to a dazzling array of deciduous and evergreen shrubs,

as well as herbaceous perennials, many of which I'd overlooked in the past. As soon as I began examining these plants more closely, I found that there was a definite domino effect: if there was one interesting, undemanding *Hydrangea paniculata* variety, there could be another and another. (I still am a collector, after all.)

In these busy times with so much calling for my attention, I am grateful for undemanding plants. And as I get older, it is comforting to think I may not be forced to move to a home with a small garden. I may simply rely more on dependable, resilient stalwarts.

MADE IN THE U.S.A.

I was surprised to discover that the first hydrangea introduced into Britain was the American *Hydrangea arborescens*, obtained by Peter Collinson from the colonies in 1736. This simple lacecap-flowered species was wildly popular until 1860, when *H. a.* 'Grandiflora', a showier variety with overblown mounded flower heads, was found in the mountains of Pennsylvania.

The name *arborescens* is a little misleading. *Arbor* means "tree," but far from tree-like, this hydrangea is practically an herbaceous perennial. The best I can tell, the name refers to the fact that this hydrangea comes from the forest, or is "of the wood." Today the most popular variety, and deservedly so, is 'Annabelle', a double with uniform globular flowers.

If you are growing *H. arborescens* for its self-reliance, you can leave these plants alone and let them make a thicket topped by tons of 5-inch flower clusters that fends for itself. If you're willing to put in just a little effort, though, you can alter

ABOVE, LEFT TO RIGHT:
I treat the reliable, native *Hydrangea arborescens* 'Annabelle' with nearly all sterile flowers as if it were semiherbaceous, and cut it back to 3 inches every other spring.

H. a. var. *radiata* is worth growing for its spectacular platinum-backed leaves.

Southeastern American *H. quercifolia* produced 'Snowflake', a variety with white double sterile florets that continue to grow and elongate until the end of summer when they turn green and pink.

PRECEDING PAGE:
Hydrangea paniculata 'Grandiflora' (at The Evergreens Cemetery in Brooklyn) has been popular for 150 years.

ABOVE, LEFT TO RIGHT:
Hydrangea paniculata 'Brussels Lace' is the first hydrangea to bloom, and by the time the other varieties are in bud, this one is already changing from white to pink.

H. p. 'Limelight' starts out chartreuse and retains a greenish cast as the flowers mature.

Like fine wine, the fading flowers of many blue *H. macrophylla* varieties age well. Most of the blue-flowered plants bloom pink in alkaline soil and blue in acidic soil.

the shape of the shrub and size of the blooms with just one pruning early in the spring. If all the stems on the plants are cut back to 3 inches above the ground, new shoots will rise from the ground to about 30 inches and be topped by enormous 12-inch flower heads. My compromise is to cut them down every other year and have the best of both worlds.

Nearly all of the *H. arborescens* varieties have grass green leaves, except *H. arborescens* subsp. *radiata*. This plant's unique leaves are very dark green on the top side and reflective platinum on the underside—the latter due to microscopic silver hairs. *H. a.* subsp. *radiata* is rare, but well worth the search.

Another American stalwart is the oakleaf hydrangea, *H. quercifolia*. Frankly, I've never met an oakleaf hydrangea I didn't like, but my preferences are for the species, or such fascinating selections as 'Snow Flake', with its conical "hose-in-hose" flowers. There are also dwarf oakleaf hydrangea varieties ('Pee Wee', 'Sykes Dwarf'); one with chartreuse leaves ('Little Honey'); and many double-flowered types—all worth seeing, many worth having. These plants offer great fall leaf color, ranging from scarlet to crimson to maroon depending on temperatures and location, and cinnamon-colored exfoliating bark for winter interest. The showy sterile flowers are creamy white, for the most part, but fade to green, pink, and chestnut brown over time.

Perhaps the best known of the white hydrangeas with floret colors that change as the blossoms age is the old standby, *H. paniculata* 'Grandiflora'. The species *H. paniculata* was introduced into England from Japan in 1861, shortly before the International Exhibition in London that set off the mania for all things Japanese (see "Japonism" on page 203). By the turn of that century, the double-flowered *H. p.* 'Grandiflora'—nicknamed the "PeeGee hydrangea," from the species' and

NIPPED IN THE BUD

Unlike *Hydrangea arborescens* and *H. paniculata,* which can both be pruned in the spring, pruning of *H. macrophylla*, bigleaf hydrangea (and the less familiar *H. serrata*), should wait until after the plant has flowered, lest you miss a season of big blue blooms. These hydrangeas blossom on last year's growth, so if they are pruned in early spring, as many people tend to do, the flower buds will be carried off to the compost pile. That is the case with *H. quercifolia*, the oakleaf, as well; I missed out on blooms three years running in the New Jersey garden thanks to winter grazing by the deer.

The pruning for bigleaf hydrangeas is fairly straightforward. In the first year of a stem's life, it shoots up succulent and green from the ground. Toward the end of the summer, a flower bud will form at the tip. The second year, if all goes well, the stem produces a large blossom at the terminal end. The stem begins to grow small side branches, which in the third year will bear smaller flowers. That year, the stem will be brown and start to have shaggy, papery bark. After this second flowering in the third year, the stem may begin to die.

If you live in a colder climate, leave the old stems to help hold up snow, and to add some wind protection for the flower buds that formed at the top of the first-year stems. If you live in a climate *without* a lot of snow or cold winds, these three-year-old sheltering stems can be cut out of the plant at ground level in the fall. Stems that have bloomed twice are all that is pruned away—none of the younger stems, and no tips on any stems.

This advice holds for hydrangeas that bloom on old growth, but that is not the case for all species. The late-blooming hydrangeas, ones that bloom after the oakleaf hydrangeas, in June to July, do so on new growth and can be pruned in early spring.

When shrubs grow too large, or become congested and twiggy and blossoming slows or ceases altogether, it may be time for renovation. Some people shear them to bring their heights down or to make them look "neat." Shearing the top off shrubs, especially older plants one hopes to renovate, will just create a thick mass of twigs that inhibit growth, and it could lead to the death of the plant. In the case of flowering shrubs, if you ask me, there are too many pruned forsythia bowling balls and tombstone azaleas in the world already.

In renovating a shrub, the first step is to cut out all dead wood—clear to the ground. If you are feeling ambitious, prune away any crossing branches, especially those scraping against each other and creating a wound where disease might enter the plant. With hydrangeas, dead stems are fairly obvious; the bark will be light in color, and the shoots will be dry and sound hollow, which they are, when you rub a stick or your loppers along the length of the stem.

For shrub renovation in general, the next step is to remove one-third of the oldest live wood, also to the ground. The next year, another third of the oldest wood can be removed, and in the third year, after you've taken stock of the fine new growth, the last of the oldest wood can be removed, if necessary. By then, all the growth should be young and fresh, and the shrub should be smaller than it was before pruning.

The general advice is to prune flowering shrubs, if necessary, right after they bloom. That can be a little hard to do to the hydrangeas, since many of them hold on to their flowers after the fresh growth ages, and they may look quite nice while they are aging. If in doubt, stick to cutting out all dead wood, and you'll be fine.

ABOVE, FROM LEFT: First-year flower buds of *Hydrangea macrophylla*. Faded flowers on three-year-old stems. Remove oldest, dead growth from the ground.

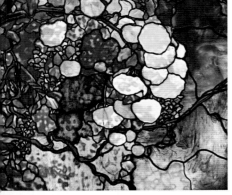

variety's initials—became ubiquitous as specimen plants in Britain. In the United States, the large shrubs, which can be trained into small trees, once graced the front yards of what seemed to be every home in America.

Now we have many *H. paniculata* selections besides the PeeGee, including *H. p.* 'Pee Wee', a miniature PeeGee; 'Limelight', which holds on to its early green flower color; and 'Brussels Lace', which blossoms earliest for me—months before 'Tardiva', a late bloomer, begins its show. My latest acquisition, discovered by Kent and Tom Buchter, is 'White Tiara' with huge panicles.

I imagine that 'White Tiara' will make its way into garden centers and onto the color pages of nursery catalogs (what some gardeners call "horticultural porn"). Perhaps this sexy plant, if not named 'PG', should at least be rated as such.

GONE BUT NOT FORGOTTEN

Louis Comfort Tiffany was a devoted gardener, and his extraordinary 1905 country estate, Laurelton Hall, in Oyster Bay, New York, was a showplace. Unfortunately, it burned down in 1957, but by then much of the contents of the house had been sold or carried away as salvage. In 2006, the Metropolitan Museum of Art presented an exhibition that included many pieces originally showcased in Laurelton Hall. One stained-glass window was described on the accompanying label as featuring wisteria and hydrangea. Most gardeners would assume that Mr. Tiffany merely indulged in a bit of artistic license, since hydrangeas were known to be among his favorites, and it is well known that these plants do not bloom at the same time. But in point of fact, Tiffany was depicting two plants that *could* be found blooming together in voluptuous profusion in May. The author of the label may be forgiven for misidentifying the hydrangea-like puffy white snowball viburnum depicted in glass, given that the once popular shrub has been all but forgotten.

Remembering the snowball from my childhood (the name alone was enough to excite a kid), I began to track down this shrub soon after moving to New Jersey. The "snowballs" I came across had flower clusters that were smaller than the ones I remembered, about the size of tennis balls. The shrubs were smaller as well, and more compact. Yet I clearly remember that the big shrub growing on the boundary line of our property had lumpy hemispherical cymes of sterile florets larger than a grapefruit. Although not a hydrangea, the similarity in bloom size and leaf shape is a strong one.

My parents built their brick ranch house in 1951 in what had been the tony part of town, where huge Victorian houses lined the streets. The house on our property had burned down, but a pride of pink-, red-, and white-flowered rhododendrons survived, as did the snowball.

THE THRILL OF THE HUNT

When I first started to search for the Chinese snowball in 2000, I could not find a source, not even with the help of the Internet. Tracking down a desired plant can be frustrating, especially if you do not know the Latin or scientific name. When you meet a plant you think you would like to acquire, do all you can to learn its actual name, and if possible where its caregiver found it. Take notes regarding specific characteristics, as well as pictures of the leaves, flowers, bark, and so on. You may be able to post them on an online garden forum.

As with almost all types of information—and shopping—the Internet has made searching for and purchasing hard-to-find plants easier than in the predigital age. But be aware that not everything you read on the Internet has been fact-checked. Always consider the source.

Libraries connected with botanic gardens or colleges and universities typically have excellent reference books that can help you in your quest. Resident horticulturists or botanists at public institutions are usually more than happy to help you identify a plant from pictures or old books. And if you don't live near a public garden or school with a good horticultural program, you can often contact experts via e-mail.

Access to reliable sources is one reason for becoming a member of a botanic garden. Frequently you will receive valuable publications and invitations to members-only lectures and workshops. But most of all, giving to a botanical garden is part of giving back to the Earth, and giving thanks for the bounty we have in our own gardens.

I was able to find the Chinese snowball's Latin name, but no mail-order source. Sometimes the best method for tracking down a must-have plant is the old-fashioned way: ask every gardener and nursery person you meet. Two years into my search for the elusive shrub I ran into a woman who owns Wilkerson Mill Gardens, a mail-order hydrangea nursery in Georgia, at a lecture at the Atlanta Botanical Garden. Although she didn't have the plants for sale, she did have some at the nursery, and she promised to propagate one for me. Two years later it arrived, and now lives happily in the New Jersey garden.

ABOVE: Gardening has its fashions, and the Chinese snowball fell out of favor.

Research led me to *Viburnum macrocephalum*, the Chinese snowball, which I imagine was the shrub Tiffany depicted, and which I've planted along the edge of the property in New Jersey. The Chinese snowball is a somewhat gangly shrub, which is one reason it was supplanted by the European snowball, *V. opulus* 'Roseum' (syn. *V. o.* 'Sterile'). A pert, smaller shrub I grow and can recommend for gardens that may not have enough room for the Chinese shrub, or for those who prefer a neater appearance, is the Japanese snowball, *V. plicatum*.

shrubs, abelia to zenobia

I wanted the Chinese snowball because it was rare, which made it all the more desirable, and because of my childhood memories. I was also upset that it had been pushed off the market by bright young things. But some plants from the good old days are still available, although they're often ignored in favor of the newest, latest, and greatest. I didn't give much thought to *Deutzia* species, for instance, until the returns were in: undemanding; uncomplicated; easy to propagate; valuable when needing a vertical element to add to a garden design; and covered with flowers—although they are small and do not last a very long time. The deutzias are "fast-growing" (with the possible exception of the dwarf 'Nikko'), but as attractive as those two words sound, bear in mind that "fast-growing"

OPPOSITE: One of the hard-to-find pink Japanese snowball varieties is *Viburnum plicatum* 'Kern's Pink' (with *Cotinus* foliage).

LEFT: A low-maintenance plant for the property boundary is *Deutzia*. A decade ago, 'Godsall Pink' ('Codsall Pink') was rare, but ease of culture and propagation has brought it back.

TOUGH LOVE

The general advice for knowing when to prune a flowering shrub is just after it blooms, which is usually just before it initiates new growth for flowers in the future. If a shrub blooms in spring, it is doing so on old growth—buds formed at the end of last growing season. In general, if it blooms summer to fall, it is probably flowering on new branch and bud formation initiated in spring. So following the flowers with cutting will be safe.

The difference between a scary, sad, or bothersome chore and a creative task is a matter of attitude and personal preference. Some people look upon pruning as work; others, as art—living sculpture. Some gardeners consider it both—those people who complain about having to clip the hedge might also be the same folks spending hours with cuticle scissors trimming their bonsai plants. In some cases, severe pruning results in a flush of new, huge "juvenile" growth. *Paulownia* and sycamore come to mind.

The idea of cutting a woody plant down to within an inch of its life may sound scary, much too radical; yet with a saw, sharpened pruner, or loppers in hand, the cuts you make can result in rejuvenated growth that will contribute to the beauty of the garden. (And no, I'm not thinking of topiary.) Willows and dogwood shrubs can be cut nearly to the ground in a process called "stooling" (the remaining stump is like a little stool) or "coppicing" (the multiple shoots that emerge below the cut make a little forest or copse). When I cut back a willow in late winter, dozens of shoots will grow up with the new growing season (some people use these new shoots to weave wattle fence or edging or even baskets).

I grow several willow and shrub dogwood varieties just for their brilliant stem colors that enliven the garden in winter. I call these varieties my "cutbacks." One- and two-year-old "whips" offer the most vivid color; therefore, every other year, I cut these specimens back—hard. Most of the brilliant willows are selections or hybrids of the same species that gives us the weeping willow (*Salix alba*, the white willow). The varieties 'Britzensis' (orange), 'Chermesina' (red), and 'Vitellina' (bright yellow) look striking against a snow-covered garden. If left alone, shrub dogwoods will grow into shrubby thickets, which makes them another low-maintenance option for hedges and screening the garden. Of course, you may

want to give them a quick spruce-up, and I've found pruning them "hard" every other year is all it takes to keep them handsome and colorful. Dogwood shrubs with colorful twigs in winter include the red-stemmed Tatarian dogwood (*C. alba*), *C. a.* 'Bloodgood', *C. a.* 'Sibirica', red osier dogwood (*C. sericea*), and *C. s.* 'Cardinal'; yellow-stemmed *C. alba* 'Bud's Yellow', *C. sanguinea* 'Silver and Gold', and *C. stolonifera* 'Flavi-ramea'; and *C. sanguinea* 'Midwinter Fire', and *C. s.* 'Midwinter Flame', which feature shifting shades from yellow to orange to red.

In my opinion, *Salix caprea,* the ubiquitous pussy willow one finds in most gardens and for sale everywhere, is not a super shrub. On the other hand, the old species *S. chaenomeloides*, a handsomely giant version with leaves like a flowering quince, blooms a full month earlier in my garden—every February, without fail—and the pussies remain perfect for more than a month, silvery and twice as large as the more familiar one. Every few years, I cut back the big shrub. Unlike the more common pussy willow, this plant does not have to be hidden around back by the garbage can and kept only for cuttings to bring into the house. Its pale green and silvery leaves make it a perfect colorful foil to flowering perennials in the foreground.

I've found that cutting back selected shrubs and trees can become part of the creative gardening routine; and fun. For the gardener interested in artistic effects, this form of extreme pruning might be the kindest cut of all.

OPPOSITE: Winter twigs of *Salix alba* 'Britzensis'. ABOVE LEFT: Rejuvenated growth of *Paulownia tomentosa*. ABOVE RIGHT: Silvery *Salix irrorata* in winter.

could equate to more frequent pruning and other maintenance. "Dwarf" and "slow" are underrated words in gardening (this latter being pejorative, except when used for grass that must be mowed).

Other descriptions that are not so good in gardening are "easy"; "carefree"; "for dummies"; "foolproof"; "goof-proof"; "deer-proof"; "spreading"; "running"; "climbing"; and any words that could be used to describe Superman ("able to leap tall buildings in a single bound"?). Good garden etiquette terms include "self-reliant"; "drought-tolerant"; "local"; "insect-resistant"; "disease-resistant"; "deer-resistant"; "fall color"; "long-lasting"; "fragrant"; "stalwart"—you get the idea.

Daring to dip a toe into the bathwater of hyperbole, however, there are quite a few old-fashioned shrubs that deliver 1,000 percent, among them the deutzia, weigela, and most of the hydrangeas. The New York City landscape designer Lyndon Miller calls these "plants that pay the rent," and she means shrubs that give back as much or more than they are given, and are worth the precious space they occupy, paying dividends for decades.

Every area has stalwarts that are particularly suited to that location: in hot climates with warmer winters, for example, many shrubs are evergreen, fewer deciduous. Plants drop their leaves in climates that have dry seasons, as well as in cold seasons. And, of course, some plants are better behaved in one area than another. A handful of shrubs should not be grown anywhere, such as burning bush (*Euonymus elata*) and green barberry (*Berberis thunbergii*).

For those of us with hot summers and cold winters, there are a surprising number of tough and rugged stalwarts from which to choose. Keep an eye out for species and varieties in the following genera: *Aesculus* (buckeye), *Aronia* (black and red chokecherry), *Calycanthus* (Carolina spicebush), *Caryopteris* (blue mist spirea), *Chaenomeles* (flowering quince), *Clethra* (sweet pepperbush), *Corylopsis* (winter hazel), *Cotinus* (smoke bush), *Exochorda* (pearlbush), *Fothergilla, Fuchsia, Hibiscus, Hypericum, Ilex* (deciduous holly), *Itea, Kalmia* (mountain laurel), *Kerria, Kolkwitzia* (beautybush), *Osmanthus* (sweet olive), *Philadelphus* (mock orange), *Physocarpus* (ninebark), *Poncirus* (hardy trifoliate orange), *Potentilla, Sambucus* (elderberry), *Symphoricarpos* (snowberry), *Syringa* (lilac), *Vaccinium* (blueberry, etc.), *Viburnum,* and *Vitex* (chaste tree), and more.

It pays to consider what these shrubs are up to today. Not all of them appear as they did generations ago, since there are new varieties of many of the plants our great-grandmothers knew. *Physocarpus opulifolius,* for example, an incredibly hardy and forgiving shrub, may feature foliage in yellow, chartreuse, bronze, and maroon as well as the original green.

Spireas have also reintroduced themselves with help from creative growers. For example, *Spiraea japonica* now appears in about a dozen chartreuse-leaved varieties. *S. j.* 'Goldflame' and 'Goldmound' were among the first ones to come on the market. The flower colors are a little hard to take, though: 'Goldflame' is a dirty lilac

and 'Goldmound' is a too-bright pink. One of the best, introduced as a low ground cover but topping out at around 20 inches, is *S. j.* 'Magic Carpet'. The new growth is amber—gorgeous with tulips 'Prinses Irene' and 'Apricot Beauty', which bloom at the same time.

S. thunbergii is rarely seen in gardens, but its small willowlike leaves on a mounding shrub provide appealing texture in a border with or without perennials. The variety *S. t.* 'Ogon' offers the bonus of golden foliage. The arching branches of both the species and the variety are covered with white flowers in spring.

One of the best-known antique shrubs is the bridal wreath, *S. × vanhouttei*, which is covered with little white, double flowers in June to July. I find this shrub to be a little too bare beneath the flowering stems, but my prejudice (which I intend to

ABOVE LEFT: *Spiraea japonica* 'Magic Carpet' is a 2-foot-tall gold-leaved variety with vivid copper new growth, and it goes perfectly with the tulip 'Prinses Irene'.

ABOVE: *Weigela subsessilis* 'Canary' blooms in partial shade and early—just after the forsythias.

ABOVE RIGHT: Twiggy *Spiraea prunifolia* (probably the selection 'Plena') has tiny double flowers on a plant that looks like a wild blooming fountain.

overcome) could be due to a much more interesting cousin of this plant being completely ignored.

S. prunifolia is an underused stalwart that blooms for about a month with dime-size, flat, double roselike flowers. In less than a half day of sunlight, the shrub stands erect, up to 6 feet. On top of all this, the autumn foliage color is stunning—yellow-orange, red, and, for me, violet and aubergine. Just to prove a point, the common name for this plant is the same as for *S. × vanhouttei*, bridal wreath. The one sold, if you can find it, is usually *S. p.* 'Plena'. If you have a good garden center, talk to the owner or manager and ask if a plant can be ordered. But be sure to have the correct name. If you have your heart set on *S. prunifolia* but receive *S. × vanhouttei*, you will know what I mean.

NOT TONIGHT, DEER

I lecture all around the country, and everywhere I go, someone will ask, "How do I keep deer out of the garden?" and "Can you give us a list of deer-proof plants?" Unfortunately we can't limit our choice of plants to a dozen or so the deer do not fancy—not only because it stifles creativity but also because the deer have proved to be unpredictable, grazing today on plants they have ignored for years. The boxwood has yet to join the list of "decimated by deer" plants, but I fear that it may be only a matter of time.

I remember reading lists of "deer-proof" plants that erroneously included roses (the deer must hate the thorns), rhododendrons (after all, these plants are poisonous), and English ivy (also toxic). At the top of every list was a very toxic plant—*Taxus*, the yew—evergreen shrubs that, in my experience, are deer bait! What deer eat in one area may be ignored by deer in another region. A Midwest Cooperative Extension Service put mountain laurel on its list of plants deer don't eat, yet entire hilltops in Connecticut have been denuded of its state flower by the animals.

I knew it was a gamble when I planted a columnar yew in the gravel garden as an accent, a botanical totem pole. Because I do not want the critters that visit daily to strip my gorgeous plant, I've wrapped the shrub in black-plastic bird netting—which is not completely invisible, but it works. I have fenced the most vulnerable parts of my property with 8-foot-tall netting, a tactic that works 97 percent of the time—until a bear tears down part of the fence, ushering the deer back in. Paradoxically, smaller fences and barriers may be as, or even more, effective.

Several years ago, I visited a vast landscaped property in Ohio where everything, including an extensive rhododendron collection, had been grazed. However, a little vegetable garden of raised beds surrounded by a 2-foot-tall fence had not been touched. *Nothing* inside of the short fence was eaten. Why? The owners did not know, but the answer reveals a bit of deer psychology.

Even though a mature deer can clear an 8-foot-high fence, it will not hazard a short hop over a 2-foot fence onto a narrow path next to a raised bed where it could possibly break a leg; deer won't jump if they can't see a clear landing place. The raised beds in this small garden were constructed out of 2x12 lumber, and the paths between the beds were only about 2 feet wide.

A similar idea is the double fence, an effective and potentially attractive solution. Betsy Clebsch, America's salvia guru, has two 4-foot-tall fences about 5 feet apart with roses growing between them. The barriers surround her intensively planted garden south of San Francisco.

As far as I can tell, all of the spray products on the market work, from predator urine, to a few potentially hazardous poisons, to garlic, rotten eggs, parsley, sage, rosemary, or thyme. But these expensive sprays must be applied regularly without fail. Switching products from time to time is also advisable—a lesson I learned the hard way.

The repellents discourage deer by having either a smell they do not like or a taste they find unpleasant, or both. The off-putting smells are better perhaps, since deer won't have to sample a plant in order to get a taste of the offending potion. But the taste deterrents may work better in cold weather when low temperatures deaden the smell. Obviously you'll want to choose a preparation that will not drive you out of the garden along with the deer. And remember, new leaves and flowers must be sprayed as soon as they appear.

The bottom line is that if a winter is harsh and there is nothing else to eat, a deer will eat any and all plants, whether or not they have been sprayed or they are allegedly poisonous. Perhaps it's time to think about getting a dog. Depending on the breed, dogs that are allowed to roam your fenced and deer-repellent-sprayed property will usually keep deer out—but not always. If you have invisible fencing to keep your dog in, it won't take long for the deer to discover the boundary, and they seem to have sadistic notions of ways to taunt the dog.

OPPOSITE: Yew (*Taxus*), a deer favorite (top); deer damage on arborvitae (bottom).
ABOVE LEFT: Deer-resistant grass, *Hakonechloa macra* 'Aureola'. ABOVE RIGHT: "Deer-pruned" topiary yew in a wire frame.

ABOVE: A traditional boxwood hedge at Greenwood Gardens in Short Hills, New Jersey. This is deer country, but the shrubs have not been touched.

ABOVE RIGHT: The hedges (*Buxus sempervirens*) at Greenwood Gardens have been sheared every year since they were planted in the 1950s. Most boxwood varieties can be rejuvenated by cutting old wood back.

comeback and can even be found at most big-box home-improvement stores (often mislabeled, I find). The resurgence might be due to baby boomers' nostalgic cravings, or perhaps a return to more formal garden design. But it is most likely due to one overriding factor: deer don't eat it.

Boxwood is being used for ground covers where deer have devoured plants such as evergreen azaleas and for hedges where the beasts have routinely de-needled evergreen yews. If the deer retain their aversion to boxwood, informal flower beds where deer tend to dine may soon give way to formal parterres with paisley patterns cut in dwarf box.

For centuries, there were two popular types of boxwood, the so-called English and so-called American boxwoods—neither of which originated in those countries, instead named for their historical associations. Most species come from the area around the Black Sea. *Buxus sempervirens* is the one familiar in American gardens up north. The variety *B. s.* 'Suffruticosa', shorter and with smaller leaves, is the widely grown "English" variety popular across the pond, and below the Mason-Dixon Line—and the choice of such gardeners as George Washington, who planted it at Mount Vernon.

But boxwoods have developed problems in some areas of the country. In the South, ancient plants the size of Volkswagens started dying in the 1980s, and young replacements soon succumbed as well. When all of the clipped English boxwood in George Washington's Pleasure Garden at Mount Vernon began to die (it is believed that they were grown from cuttings of Washington's original plants), Dean Norton, Mount Vernon's director of horticulture, suggested they be replaced with another variety. But historians insisted that the replacements be the same English boxwood Washington grew. Therefore, 2,500 identical plants were purchased and installed. And 2,500 plants died. The dead plants were removed, all the soil dug up and carted away, and another 2,500 English box were planted, again. When those plants started to die, and the cost was nearing $60,000, the historians conceded.

Few diseases attack boxwood, and seemingly only certain species and cultivars succumb, and only in some locations around the country. One problem is boxwood decline, caused by fungal diseases that attack the English variety. Symptoms begin with browning leaves, followed by the sudden death of sections of shrub, and ultimately, the loss of the entire plant. There is no cure.

Cultural experiments with boxwood have led to some new advice for avoiding the disease. Boxwood specialist Paul Saunders, founder of Saunders Brothers Nursery and coordinator of the National Boxwood Trials, recommends planting high. Unlike most nursery-grown plants, Saunders says boxwood should be put in the ground so that the root flare, the point where the stem or trunk begins to grow wider and roots emerge, should be situated nearly an inch *above* the soil level.

Dr. Lynn R. Batdorf of the National Arboretum, considered this country's expert on box, suggests maintaining a 1-inch-thick mulch around the plants, not much more, not much less. He also says that severing shallow roots when edging beds too close to a boxwood can likewise cause decline and death. Experts further advise against shearing boxwood growing in sunny sites, which encourages thick growth on the outside of the plant, which in turn blocks light from reaching the inner leaves. Excessive outer growth also reduces air circulation and encourages infections of *Volutella* canker, which kills foliage and entire branches. Thinning plants—pruning out branches right down to the trunks of the plants—is the recommended alternative for renovating shrubs or reducing their size (see "Tough Love" on page 228).

Boxwood wants an alkaline or "sweet" soil, pH 6.5 to 7.2. Proper soil alkalinity greatly improves growth rate and the general health of the plants. Afternoon shade, particularly in the South, reduces boxwood mite infestations.

In the boxwood trials, various public and private gardens planted and reported on varieties in different parts of the country. For naturally upright growth, 'Dee Runk' and 'John Baldwin' were recommended. I have had great success with *B. sempervirens* 'Graham Blandy', the narrowest of the cultivars, but apparently in warmer climates it is prone to disease. People buy these naturally narrow cultivars for hedges, but that seems odd to me. Why not buy plants that grow wider and prune them when necessary? The narrow ones will never fill in, and they will cost much more money since so many more plants will be needed. I think when dealing with a plant that looks like an exclamation point, it should be used just like the punctuation would be: to make an emphatic design statement!

Suggested medium-size plants include *B. sinca* var. *insularis* 'Justin Brouwers', variegated *B. sempervirens* 'Elegantissima', *Buxus* 'Glencoe' hybrid (syn. 'Chicagoland Green'), and *B. microphylla* var. *japonica*. The large plants include the best overall

RIGHT: *Buxus sempervirens* 'Elegantissima' is pruned into an urn-shaped topiary in my garden (top); 'Graham Blandy' is a naturally columnar variety of boxwood (center); some *Buxus* cultivars have bright green new growth for up to a month in spring (bottom).

boxwood for the North and much of the country, the species *B. sempervirens*, and *B. s.* 'Inglis'. Among the dwarf choices are *B. microphylla* 'Grace Hendrick Phillips' and 'Morris Dwarf'.

From what I have observed, American boxwood, the species *B. sempervirens*, is the sturdiest of all. Experts at Ladew Topiary Gardens in Maryland clip hemlock and yew but think boxwood is the best for creating a shaped plant that needs the least frequent pruning or major renovation. I grow *B. s.* 'Elegantissima', a slower-growing, variegated form with smaller gray-green leaves than the species, edged in creamy yellow. Mine is pruned into the shape of an antique oil jar, a formal element in my informal gravel garden. I prune it once as new growth is beginning and do a touch-up trim in August.

Like many people, I find boxwood smell objectionable. The unpleasant odor holds the key to boxwood's comeback. The deer will not prune boxwood, but a gardener may clip it into nearly any shape, and it will sprout from an endless supply of dormant leaf buds. Perhaps the most fitting living sculpture might be a topiary clipped into a fleeing deer.

Back at Washington's Mount Vernon, Paul Saunders advised Dean Norton to plant 'Morris Dwarf', named for the Morris Arboretum near Philadelphia. By 2006, three years after planting, not one of the 'Morris Dwarf' shrubs had died. The ancient boxwood has been highly prized for centuries, and it will no doubt rise in stature in the future. As for my nose, I am learning to tolerate the smell, and tolerance is a big step toward acceptance.

PERENNIAL FAVORITES

Like the old-fashioned self-reliant shrubs, there are herbaceous perennials that I need tend to only once or twice in a season; once these plants have become established, I can depend on them to take care of themselves. Also like the self-reliant shrubs, some of these herbaceous perennials are nostalgic favorites (Ostrich fern, *Matteuccia struthiopteris*), some are overlooked (bear's breeches, *Acanthus hungaricus*), and still others have taken on a legendary status among gardeners the world over.

What plant becomes a legendary herbaceous perennial? Consider a plant such as the delphinium, for instance. These gorgeous long-legged beauties with single or double flowers on narrow spikes up to 7 feet tall by variety are always favorites—especially when they are blue. Can you grow this plant? Very few people who live in places where summer temperatures climb above 80 degrees F can, and yet for many gardeners delphiniums are dearer than the Holy Grail.

I admit that I've come to resent plants like the delphinium that—after I've given my heart and soul over to them—disappear over winter, leaving just a white plant label, like a little grave marker. Still other herbaceous garden plants present a bit of a challenge and need coddling, which they may deserve.

OPPOSITE, CLOCKWISE FROM TOP LEFT:
Alchemilla mollis blooms with frothy chartreuse flowers late spring into summer; it is a great low-maintenance, fill-in plant.

Peonies take the word "perennial" to heart. Provided the roots are planted with their growing eyes between 1 and 2 inches below the soil surface, they will bloom for a century. The ostrich fern, like most ferns, is not attractive to deer.

Hostas (like 'Tattoo') can grow into ground-covering drifts, but they are far from immune to grazing animals.

On the other hand, *Delphinium* are very poisonous, and critters know it. The challenge is defying the heat that most U.S. gardens experience. Recent New Zealand hybrids have been bred to tolerate very warm and humid summers.

So, what becomes an herbaceous perennial? The right soil, temperature, moisture, luck, and often the guiding hand of a gardener are what it takes to make these plants thrive. But if I am going to pay extra attention to some perennials such as new hosta introductions, others will have to care for themselves. The herbaceous perennials that serve as stalwarts in my garden are able to do just that.

Once established, these plants increase in size, not by spreading to pop up in places far afield from their planting site but by enlarging their clumps into patches. Although they do not have to be divided to thrive or bloom, as a rule, neither do they resent being divided, and that is one way to help them fill their intended spaces. Most of them are not bothered by insects or disease, and many tend to escape browsing by deer.

I can't generalize and say all species and varieties in one genus will behave as I hope, or that they will perform for every gardener as they do for me. For instance, *Stachys byzantina* 'Helene von Stein' displays these qualities, and unlike the more common lamb's ears, this one also called 'Big Ears' rarely flowers, and therefore rarely disintegrates like its common cousin. The stachys is more of a subshrub than a traditional herbaceous perennial, having more permanent stems and being semievergreen. Another example might be the genus *Ligularia*. These plants in general are slug and snail bait, plain and simple, but a recent discovery, *L. japonica,* has formed a welcome stand next to the canal, where it shares residence with thousands of snails, and yet the finely incised palmate leaves remain unmarred. This plant is happy, but in a drier spot or one with more direct sunlight, I doubt it would do as well.

The popular *Rudbeckia* 'Goldsturm' might come to mind as clump forming, but if rabbits visit your garden, you will never see these plants. Ornamental grasses are rarely browsed, but dividing some of them takes a chain saw or a backhoe. Other plants that can fill an area in a polite but complete way are the *Phlox paniculata* selections; these can be disfigured by mildew, however, which is unattractive but ultimately harmless. An old suggestion was to grow a lot of different varieties and to keep the ones that did not suffer in your garden. You could also talk to a neighbor and compare notes. While you're at it, look for *Phlox* 'David'. There are probably gardeners out there who have trouble with this super-clean white-flowered variety, but I have not met them.

As much as I can recommend plants that have worked for me, and probably will work for you in a similar climate, you have to discover some of the species and varieties on your own in the place where you live. For example, lupines will work perfectly for some gardeners in some climates, but in other places, they are next to impossible to grow. The taller kinds, for instance, thrive where winters are cold and summers cool. Look to local public gardens and the plantings of friends. What are the candidates that make well-behaved, contained little colonies? It may be hard to know for sure just by looking, however, so ask. Gardeners will be more than happy to share some of the discoveries they have made, suggest sources, and, if you're lucky, share a few plants as well.

drifts and sweeps and rivers

In 2005, I was inspired to try out a new design concept in the garden. I wanted to bring a more cohesive look to the beds with repetitions of perennials—massed plantings of one species or variety—that would flow like streams, connecting one planted area to another. I started my plan with plants that I already grow, the ones that I know can easily be divided to make more, such as *Hosta sieboldiana* 'Elegans'. Although I don't like to call these perennials fillers, I chose them because they have just the right way of taking up space and plugging gaps.

As the plantings established themselves, I began to notice that the plants I'd chosen not only succeeded at weaving streams of color and texture, many of them also suppressed weeds, effectively serving as ground covers and saving me hours of weeding. Success encouraged me to use more of these plants in more general ways, to fill in beyond the flower border. When I think of a ground cover, I picture a plant that is no more than 6 inches tall, but as I've learned, any plant that covers the ground is one, even azaleas or sumac. The hostas did this job, and if they were not such notorious critter magnets, I would use them in more places. The hostas can, however, withstand cold winters and unexpected droughts. Freed from tending the areas of the garden where these plants grow, I've been able to dote on beds where other plants reside, including the ones that need quite a bit of attention—like the delphinium I raised from seeds bought online from a New Zealand seed source. A Pittsburgh acquaintance had turned me on to the New Zealand delphinium after he had quite a bit of success through the hot summers we share.

I now find myself seeking out more of these ground-covering stalwarts and ones, unlike the hostas, that are not bothered by pests. I recently discovered *Acanthus hungaricus*, bear's breeches, sometimes listed as *A. balcanicus* var. *hungaricus*. The glossy leaves are deeply lobed, thistlelike, and deep green. In summer, 3-foot-tall spikes appear with buds that open into stiff flowers in shades of eggplant purple, white, and dark green, with threadlike veining. They look like giant snapdragons or turtleheads and remain fresh for a long time. In their stalwart manner, they even remain attractive as they begin to fade, and I don't bother removing the dead flower spike until they have turned completely brown. The acanthus, knock wood, have not been bothered by insects or mammals, so far, although adjacent plants have been nibbled into oblivion.

Plants of the genus *Epimedium* are more conventional ground covers for semi-shaded spots, growing 10 to 15 inches by species and variety. The wild gingers, named for the fragrance of their crushed leaves, are very low-growing, 3 inches or less. Once I discovered the secret to getting these members of the genus *Asarum* to cover

OPPOSITE: Perennial stalwarts *Stachys lanata* 'Helene von Stein' (top); snail-resistant *Ligularia japonica* flowers with sumac 'Tiger Eyes' foliage (center); and *Phlox paniculata* 'David', which is mildew free for me (bottom).

ABOVE: Future garden plants *Baptisia* 'Carolina Moonlight' (top) and *B. perfoliata* (above).

more ground faster, they proved perfect for creating drifts and sweeps in semishaded to shaded areas. Decades ago, I transplanted a lush specimen of European ginger (*A. europeum*) from a 1-gallon pot that it had completely filled. After it was planted out in the garden, the ginger remained in the same tight circle it had grown in for years. I am not sure what led me to divide it, but I did, into quite small pieces, and it took off. The same thing may work with a tight clump of lungwort (*Pulmonaria*).

Like the acanthus, the lungwort around the garden has not been eaten, and like the wild ginger, dividing it encourages it to spread its wings. Each piece becomes as large as the original plant in a year or two and, depending on spacing, can form a carpet of foliage and spring flowers. Some of the species and varieties of lungwort suffer from mildew, but others do not, and those should be sought. You may find selections of *Pulmonaria vallarsae*, *P. saccharata*, *P. longifolia*, *P. angustifolia*, and *P. rubra* on the market, and hybridists and growers are always coming up with new ones that seem to be quite mildew-resistant.

Lungworts feature wide variations in leaf color and shape. Midspring flowers are usually blue but can also be white or pink. Most of these plants have fuzzy leaves, some plain green, others spotted silver, and a few completely silver. In general, the silver-leaved selections need more sunlight. After the plants bloom in midspring, the leaves on some of the varieties, for example, the sensational mildew-free selection 'Majeste', turn black at the edges, then crinkle and roll, and often look horrible. My friend Heidi Hamilton told me to cut the plant back "hard," which I did timidly at first, and it pushed a flush of gorgeous new leaves that remained pristine until frost. A plant that needs to be cut back sounds like it might be bumped from a list of stalwarts, but a ten-minute operation is not very much to ask for all that the plant returns.

For edging a bed or border, nothing beats lady's mantle, *Alchemilla mollis*. There are a few other tiny-leaved species that are well suited for the rock garden (*A. alpina*, for example), but lady's mantle, with its neat mounds of gold green leaves, shaped a bit like a geranium's, is among the old reliables. The leaves are covered with tiny hairs that make them waterproof, and when it rains, water will form a bead and settle in the center of the leaf or hug the edges, adding sparkle to the dense foliage. The leaves are great, yes, but the plant is at its best when it is in flower. Clouds of tiny chartreuse flowers rise above the foliage and last for about a month. The acid green flowers and gray foliage are fantastic together. This alchemilla will make a somewhat oval, very tight clump, and to get it to grow in a line hugging the bed edge, you'll need more plants, and those can be had by dividing the plants. I cannot claim that this is effortless—you may need a saw. And like many plants that work for me, lady's mantle is not for everyone. Marcia Donahue, a sculptor and gardener in Berkeley, California, says it poops out for her—too much shade, I suspect.

Dry shade, poor soil, and rocky areas are among the gardener's daunting challenges, and if these spots are also weedy, finding perennials to fill the gaps is not

OPPOSITE, CLOCKWISE FROM TOP LEFT: Weed-suppressing groundcover big-root geranium (*Geranium macrorrhizum*), beneath wisteria.

Big-root geranium's fragrant foliage develops fall color.

G. 'Rozanne' blooms all season long.

Pulmonaria rubra has no pests.

Flowers of 7-foot-tall *Thalictrum rochebrunianum* look of butterflies.

Ground-covering, foot-tall *Astilbe chinensis* var. *pumila*.

Winter-flowering, pest-resistant hellebore.

North American "closed" or "bottle gentian," *Gentiana andrewsii*.

OPPOSITE, CENTER: Useful woodland newcomer *Anemone nemorosa* 'Bracteata Pleniflora', with double white flowers and green bracts, remains ornamental for months.

easy. In partial shade (say, four hours of sun or more), *Geranium macrorrhizum* (another subshrub like lamb's ear), will do the job.

Of course, preparing the area, clearing away weeds before planting, is still a good idea. *Macrorrhizum* means "big root," but it is really a stem in this case that suggests the specific epithet. When a little sunlight strikes the plants, there will be a pleasant scent of cinnamon and raisins. If bruised, the felted and grayish green leaves release much more fragrance, as I've discovered when accidently stepping on them while trying to reach a nearby plant. The geranium does not seem to be bothered, or else it just repairs itself quickly; in fact, if a brittle stem breaks off, and they do, you can stick the broken end in the ground and it will root in. The leaves take on wonderful fall colors, but the deep pink flowers in late spring are not the easiest

ABOVE: More plants to use en masse: purple pineapple lily (*Eucomis* 'Sparkling Burgundy'– hardy to 10°F) introduced by Plant Delights Nursery (left); *Hosta sieboldiana* 'Elegans' along the woodland path (center); true stalwart and surprisingly absent from most gardens is the long-blooming herbaceous *Acanthus hungaricus* (right).

color to like. There are varieties, however; the white version, 'Alba', is lovely, but it does not grow as quickly or densely as the species. The density of the growth is the key. The species has not spread beyond its initial unforgiving site, on rocks with a bit of soil, yet it suppresses weeds like no other.

Deer have yet to eat my hellebores, plants that will thrive in sun and also in dry partial shade. The handsome, deep green leaves of the Oriental hybrids, *Helleborus* × *hybridus*, are palmate, and the plants grow to about a foot in height. Although the ferny-leaved astilbes are also resistant to four-legged creatures, I do not love them equally. Some of the plume-topped raspberry-colored flowering varieties are all right, I suppose, in partial shade; however, there are more exciting varieties such as *Astilbe chinensis* var. *pumila*, which is topped in summer by stiff,

fuzzy, lavender-pink flowers and makes a dense weed-suppressing mat and a good connector in the garden. *Pumila* means "dwarf," and the plants are. *A. simplicifolia* 'Sprite' is even smaller, with more familiar airy dark pink flowers. I grow this one with the micro *Aruncus aethusifolius*, which it much resembles. In flower, however, the tiny *Aruncus*, or goatsbeard, is cream colored and looks like a 4-inch-tall version of its 4-foot-tall "ground-cover" cousin, *Aruncus dioicus*.

More like feathers than ferns, *Amsonia hubrectii* is a great "new" plant that is on the verge of overexposure. But there are solid reasons this plant, a southeastern U.S. native, has skyrocketed to the height of fashion. This version of bluestar, which I first saw in a native-plant garden in its North Carolina homeland, has clusters of periwinkle blue flowers in the spring on 2-foot-tall stems covered with threadlike green leaves. After two or three years, a few plants will form a nice clump. Fall color is unusual in perennials, and this makes the thread-leaf bluestar stand out among its peers. The leaves turn from green to brilliant yellow, pink, and orange—transforming into clouds of color that glow when ignited by the low shafts of autumn sunlight.

There are many, many other plants to cultivate as low-maintenance herbaceous perennials that will knit themselves through your garden without overtaking it. Your location will determine which are best for your circumstances, and your own experience has probably suggested a few already. Growing dozens of undemanding plants, as you can see, does not mean settling for boring plants. Like everyone else, I gravitate toward plants that catch my eye. Some fend for themselves, others are quite demanding (and some are now dead). I can't help myself. But these days, I also ask, "Are you going to help care for yourself?" Hearing that the answer is "no" won't stop me (plants are notorious fibbers, and I am no stranger to denial). In most cases, I have to try to find out for myself.

INTO THE WOOD

I love trees, and I admit to having hugged a few in my day. And, although I may take the time to stroke the smooth bark of the Japanese maple in the garden, a tree that I know is well into its second century, I realize that not everyone regards trees with such reverence.

Around the first of the year in 2007, I saw bulldozers scraping away yet another hillside in my county, which was rural when I moved here in 1995. A great old oak stood at the top of the rise, and the developers, aware of the big tree's monetary value, were planning to spare it. I suppose it is a good sign that at the very least they didn't cut down the tree, even though the motive was far from altruistic.

What is a gorgeous old tree worth? It's hard to say, unless one needs an insurance value for replacement. The cost of a mature tree varies according to variety and age of the specimen. A tree dug from an old nursery could cost around $1,000 per caliper-inch above 12 inches (measured at 1 foot up the trunk from the ground). A 15-inch-diameter tree, therefore, which could easily be over 25 feet tall, would go for about $15,000. The price may include planting. Cranes are often involved with larger trees, or sometimes helicopters airlift giant megaton root balls.

To get the attention of the people who most endanger the trees, to get to their hearts, it may be necessary to go through their wallets. I don't think folks would cut down trees as easily as they do if they knew they were worth 20 grand or more. Trees increase property values for home owners. Trees produce shade, lowering air-conditioning costs, and act as windbreaks, which can reduce heating bills as well. Trees fight wind and water erosion, and clean the air, and lock carbon in their wood until it is burned or processed and released back into the atmosphere. And for those who may see only the bottom line, timberland has outperformed the stock market for the last 30 years, generating increases in average annual returns of 14.5 percent.

The crew working on the site of the old oak, despite good intentions, didn't seem to realize that trees do not appreciate having their roots run over 50 or 60 times by bulldozers. Scraping down the mound of earth where the tree's roots grow to the shape of an apple core seals the deal. It may take three or more years for the tree to die, but die it will.

Seeing this kind of poorly informed action is painful. Sometimes I suspect I have chlorophyll coursing through my veins. When a plant hurts, I hurt a little too. After all, these are the subjects of my affection and passion, and it seems natural, or even necessary, to empathize with the living things in my care—in order to care for them better. I'm not talking about tomatoes and sweet corn here. There is obviously a big difference between harvesting a crop and felling a 2,000-year-old redwood. But there are times when a tree has to be cut down, perhaps when it is ailing, or listing dangerously and hanging over the house roof.

I owe the garden for the pleasure it has given me, and I owe the Earth for the comfort I have taken from it. The best way I can pay off my debt, and hope to balance the impact I have had on the environment, is to become an advocate for plants—especially local plants—and trees most of all, which are the biggest, oldest life forms on the planet.

RESTLESS NATIVES

There are remnants of the woodland that once blanketed the valley where the New Jersey island garden grows, and a few old trees still stand, although none are as old as the foundations of the pair of one-lane bridges, the first of which was built in 1756, that pass onto and off the island.

I've taken a tree inventory of the indigenous species, old and young, that still stand within a 2,000-foot radius of the garden. I have to admit, the results surprised me. One can still see examples of maple species (box elder, red, silver, and sugar maples); oaks (white, chestnut, red, and pin oak); American beech; black willow; aspen; ironwood; Eastern red cedar; larch; tulip tree; black cherry; shagbark hickory and its cousins pignut and bitternut; sweet and gray birch; black walnut; American linden; hemlock; American elm; white ash; honey locust; Eastern white pine; and sycamore.

At the tip of the island garden stands a large sycamore tree, *Platanus occidentalis*, also called the American plane tree. The sycamore is a great plant—most of the time. The leaves are shaped like a maple's, but fuzzy and less uniform in size. In the spring, after the tree's odd fruits shatter and seeds take to the wind, the leaves emerge, or attempt to. The sycamore is highly susceptible to anthracnose, a group of fungal diseases. If the fungus isn't too bad, some leaves turn patchy brown and a few may fall. But in bad years this tree drops every single disfigured leaf. In a week or two, leaves emerge again. In a year with weather that favors the fungus, rainy and cool, the cycle of making and losing leaves may occur three times or more. Unfortunately, sycamores like the same weather conditions as do the fungi. I've

ABOVE: The part of New Jersey where my garden lives has the most species of dragonflies and darning needles in North America.

OPPOSITE, TOP TO BOTTOM: Trees are precious, especially old specimens. I stroke the smooth bark of the century-old Japanese maple in my garden whenever I pass.

This old native sycamore (*Platanus occidentalis*) grows beside the water, leaning over the river. For balance, the tree cantilevered a large branch away from the bank.

The hybrid London plane tree has bark that looks like camouflage. In winter, the sycamore's mottled, exfoliating bark reveals smooth celadon "skin."

PRECEDING PAGE: The red-leaf Japanese maple in autumn.

read that most trees cannot live through more than three refoliations in a season, but the sycamore bravely puts up with whatever nature dishes out (knock on the old trunk's wood).

The sycamore growing on the bank of the river across from the island leans out over the water at an acute and somewhat alarming angle. To balance this bit of acrobatics, it has grown a huge branch in the opposite direction, away from the river, as a natural cantilever. The tree has also sent a major section of exposed root-like trunk up the hill away from the river, which makes the sycamore look very much like a mottled hippopotamus lolling on the bank.

Through the summer, the sycamore's bark looks like camouflage, with patches of brown, tan, and green. In the winter, the exfoliated bark reveals a layer of platinum "skin"—a spectacular sight when the winter sunlight strikes the smooth metallic hide. I feel blessed to be able to witness the seasons of the sycamore tree, even while I worry about it. Will it survive three sets of refoliations, or floods when the trunk is submerged beneath 6 feet of moving water? So far, the sycamore bravely answers "yes."

I wonder what the old tree has seen through its life, as its home ground has changed. The sycamore has had an old mill and an apple tree orchard for neighbors, and now, in a battleground in the war against invasive plants, it must put up with hostile neighbors. I'll do what I can, keep down the weeds, clear off the horizontal trunk, and send good thoughts in the old tree's direction. There isn't much else I can do, I'm afraid. And I won't be spraying fungicide next to the river for the anthracnose, of that I'm certain. I just hope we both can make it through the next 40 years or so (and refoliate when necessary).

think local

I've seen a bald eagle flying over the river, and two golden eagles high above the garden, passing through the warm current of air that rises from the land between the branches of the river. On the first evening in March or April when the temperature touches 60 degrees F, the peepers—tree frogs—begin to sing in an annual chorus that continues for nearly a month. Every summer evening at dusk, when the color of the trees turns from leafy green into black silhouette, there is a bat ballet, when the creatures swoop in circles around the open cropped meadow, diving for insects. There are muskrats, mink, and, most recently, an incredibly rare fisher was sighted. I've been told by the local office of the Nature Conservancy that the area around this valley has the widest diversity of dragonflies and darning-needle species in North America.

The road in front of my house dips sharply into the valley and rises again at an angle that was too steep for horse-and-buggies and wagons in the old days. A 2-mile-long road was built to loop around the valley, and at the shady end where

ABOVE: A green frog that was iridescent turquoise once visited my garden.

OPPOSITE, CLOCKWISE FROM TOP LEFT: Some plants in my area at the base of the Appalachian mountain range include the local red columbine, *Aquilegia canadensis*.

Trillium erectum is the species growing at the base of the rock by the river, and in my woodland garden with pink *Geranium maculatum*.

The familiar jack-in-the-pulpit, *Arisaema triphyllum*, in John Gwynn's shaded Rhode Island garden.

This golden ragwort (*Packera aurea*, syn. *Senecio aureus*) is at Mt. Cuba Center in Delaware.

the aptly named Old Stagecoach Road crosses the river, there is a rock about two stories tall and 75 feet in circumference. Gratefully, the big rock proved too large an obstacle when the road and a bridge were built; and later, the railroad tracks were laid. And so it remains today, with the road jogging around it. In addition to its size, the rock is in its own way important and remarkable. Cracks in the stone are home to a living catalog of woodland wildflowers that have inhabited this neighborhood for thousands of years.

When I first saw this outcropping, native columbine grew in the rock crevices and some 50 jack-in-the-pulpit plants sprouted on the ground around it. Evergreen Christmas ferns also enjoyed the dry, shady location. In the more moist soil nearby, false hellebores (*Veratrum viride*) grew freely, as did the white wake-robin trillium (*Trillium erectum*).

The rock's rich native-plant community represents an interesting phenomenon. Ecologists say that "the edge is where the action is." Places where two types of habitats bump into each other are often the richest in diverse species, such as the riparian edge where water meets land and transitional plants live along with amphibians, reptiles, birds, and mammals. The edge of the woodland is another example, when in open spots moisture, sunlight, and soil introduce the meadow with seasonal grasses and forbs (nongrass flowering plants). In the transitional, half-shaded edge, plants such as blueberries and deciduous rhododendrons grow. But think of any place like these edges, for example, the cracks in the sidewalk choked with weeds, and where the driveway meets the lawn, an active spot for unwanted plants. The big rock on the riverbank covered with native plants was one such in-between spot.

One would think that a place like that big rock outcropping—with flora that had survived for thousands of years, or longer, and had been saved from browsing deer by the river on one side and by its own "uselessness" from a developer's point of view—would be immune to change. But ten years after I first explored the rock by the river, more than half of the local plants were gone. Much of the rock today is covered by myrtle, *Vinca minor*, and English ivy, *Hedera helix*—exotic, invasive plants from nearby gardens that escaped into the area and now threaten to overtake the micro-community completely.

To preserve these native plant species, and afford them a safe haven away from marauding garden thugs, I grow plants that I know to be "local" on a section of the island. These are plants that grow within a 10-mile radius of the property, and I've welcomed them (back) into my woodland garden beds. By including planting storehouses of local plants, we are contributing to the preservation of local species, perhaps even protecting them from total extinction. And if the time ever comes, the protected genetic material will be available to replant the woodland understory where these plants once thrived.

TREES FROM SEEDS

The Osage orange was brought to my area hundreds of years ago from the Midwest, and these trees were planted as hedgerows and to supply material for long-lasting fence posts. Cutting them back to harvest posts also encouraged the plants to shoot up dense, straight whips for barriers or, if allowed to grow, more fence posts. These plantings gave rise to another common name for this tree, hedge apple. Today the gnarled trunks and craggy bark of older trees are used by some artists for making rustic furniture able to withstand the elements. For the sake of ecological clarity, this species is not as durable as its wood—I only know of one nearby—the last half dozen having been felled in 2007. So I'm growing more.

Growing trees from seed is a challenge, but it can, with nature's help, be done. The first thing is to acquire the seed. Don't go collecting thousands of seeds that might have either germinated on their own or been food for wildlife. A dozen seeds of most trees should be enough. The seeds will then have to be removed from their various packages.

I gather seeds of most trees in the fall, but a few, among them red maple and most birch species, are ready to sow soon after flowering in spring. Nearly all plants use some type of mechanism to keep their seeds from sprouting at the wrong time and in the wrong place. A lack of moisture is one reason, but other mechanisms include chemicals in dry fruit seed coats. Moist fruit has to be removed, either by being eaten away by animals, decomposed by fungi, or cleaned away by the gardener.

Dry fruits include papery maple "helicopters," beechnuts, and pea-relative pods such as the honey locust's. There are moist fruits as well, juicy ones like black cherry, and Osage orange with its pulpy chartreuse softball-size fruit, smelling of spice, and fissured like a brain. I like to gather some from the ground to display indoors for a week or two before returning them to the place where I found them and keeping one for its seeds.

Some seeds need to be exposed to light and are sown on the soil's surface; others need darkness and should be buried below soil level. Most seeds need to be just beneath the surface, a depth equal to their thickness. (You can find more specific information in my book *Making More Plants*.)

Once I've gathered my seeds, and removed the fruit if applicable, I fill 3- or 4-inch-square plastic pots to the top with a humus-based sowing medium such as coir and perlite, press it down, and add a bit more to bring the mix just below the pot's rim. Larger seeds may be pushed into the medium, smaller ones scattered on the surface. Then the surface is covered with a sprinkling of chicken grit (granite flakes available at feed-supply stores, or parakeet gravel from the supermarket). Moisten the pots from below by setting them in a pan of water until the near-white grit darkens. Label the pots with the genus and species, the location of the harvest, and the date of when they were sown.

I either place the pots in plastic bags that go into the refrigerator until March or place them outdoors where they will be protected from strong winds and foraging animals but open to the snow or rain. A wooden box with drainage holes or a bottom and cover made of one-quarter-inch hardware cloth works well.

When the pots from the refrigerator come out, they must be placed indoors under fluorescent lights or very bright sunlight. The time it takes for these seeds to germinate depends on the species. Seedlings are transplanted when they have their first "true leaves," the set of leaves that grow after the first, or "seed leaves." Slide the contents of a pot on its side, and carefully pry up the seedlings, gently holding them by one true leaf, and move them to their new digs in individual pots, which for trees should be tall but not wide, so the seedlings can put down their taproot and will not drown in waterlogged medium.

When the danger of frost has passed, the seedlings can be moved outdoors, following acclimatization, or hardening off. This process involves taking the seedlings outside for one hour the first day, two the second, and so on until they can be left outdoors. Container-grown trees can be nurtured until they are ready to be transplanted to their permanent homes in your yard or garden, and in those of friends who want to help grow air for everyone.

OPPOSITE: Ornamental *Maclura pomifera* fruits. ABOVE: Dogwood tree seedlings. Dump the pot and transplant holding a true leaf. Water into new medium in an individual pot.

STILL GROWING AFTER ALL THESE YEARS

The British scientist and explorer Charles Darwin coined the phrase *living fossil* to describe the ginkgo, a tree that is virtually identical today to a 240-million-year-old fossilized specimen found in China. The term *living fossil* is now applied to any organism that resembles its prehistoric ancestors.

Unlike the sycamore on my property, ginkgo trees are resistant to diseases, insects, and damage from drought or excessive moisture, and they are tolerant of various soil types. The ginkgo is "monotypic," a genus with only one species. But although there is only a lone species, *Ginkgo biloba*, this single example has survived to become, by all definitions, a champion among stalwarts. Ginkgo trees growing a mile from ground zero in Nagasaki survived the atomic blast of 1945.

How old are they? The ginkgo was on the planet before the evolution of flowering plants. Although their leaves make one think of broad-leaved hardwood trees, ginkgoes are actually deciduous conifers—gymnosperms (meaning they bear naked seeds), like pines, spruce, and fir. Their closest relatives are probably the prehistoric cycads, palmlike plants with leathery leaves.

As for nomenclature, *Ginkgo biloba* is a blend of East and West languages. *Ginkgo* comes from the Japanese mispronunciation of the Chinese word for "silver apricot," *yin-kuo. Biloba* is Latin for "two-lobed": the fan-shaped ginkgo leaf is split in the middle.

The common name for *Ginkgo* is maidenhair tree, a reference to the *Adiantum* species, maidenhair ferns, with fan-shaped leaflets.

Ginkgoes are dioecious (having separate male and female individuals). In Asia, the female ginkgoes are prized for their seeds, which are considered a delicacy. Americans, on the other hand, shun the malodorous harvest. When the 1-inch round fruits ripen and fall to the ground, they exude an odor reminiscent of vomit. Fruit-littered sidewalks can make walking under a female ginkgo an unpleasant experience. Consequently, American gardeners, as well as town and city managers, consider the male ginkgoes more desirable as a street tree. Nonetheless, it is a familiar sight to see Asian women gathering ginkgo fruits for their seeds along Seventh Avenue in the Park Slope neighborhood of Brooklyn, New York. Somehow or other, the girl ginkgoes got mixed in with the boy ginkgoes at shipping time.

The ginkgo trees' tolerance of pollution, disease, and insects and their ability to thrive despite restricted root area make them perfect candidates for planting along sidewalks and streets. A beautiful specimen in Newton, New Jersey, is a stunning showstopper every autumn when the branches, like arms thrown wide against the clear blue sky, are covered in shining yellow foliage. When young, ginkgo trees grow straight up and tall, another advantage for street planting, but as they mature, the branches begin spreading wide.

The ginkgo has a nearly endless supply of dormant buds, which means the tree can be pruned to nearly any size, over and over, and it will always push new growth. The buds make the ginkgo a subject for bonsai. Visitors to the garden of Dr. Nick Nicou, a woody-plant collector in Connecticut, are usually surprised when they see his "dwarf" ginkgo, a little hemisphere less than 2 feet tall. In fact, Dr. Nicou is pulling the wool over visitors' eyes; his ginkgo is not a dwarf. He prunes the tree into a little shrub every year, and has been doing so for some 30 years.

extreme sports

Although *monotypic,* having only one species in the genus, some such cultivars have been selected as seedlings for their desirable traits. A few have extra-narrow silhouettes, making them good for tight spaces like city streets, for instance 'Mayfield', 'Princeton Sentry', and 'Fastigiata'. I have a lovely "fishtail" variety called 'Saratoga' with long leaves split down the center. My pet among the ginkgo varieties in the New Jersey garden, however, is one with compact growth and tubular leaves. When the leaves emerge in the spring, they are chautreuse and rolled almost like little horns. This small tree (kept even more bushy and dense through pruning) is trained over a large rock. I prune it about three times during the season, cutting branch stems back by 4 or 5 inches to an outward-facing bud—a delightful bit of sculpting that takes about ten minutes at a triannual clip.

The plant's name is in question. It could be 'Todd's Broom', which itself is listed in various references as 'Todd's Witches Broom' and just plain 'Todd'. This cultivated variety has to be propagated vegetatively and is usually grafted. It did not originate from seed but as aberrant growth on a branch, a mutation called a "sport" or, in the vernacular, a "witches'-broom," for the appearance of the growth. Some of these aberrations may have environmental causes such as mite attacks or fungal diseases. Others are genetic mutations in buds that grow differently from the rest of the plant. If not removed from the parent, they may sap its energy. But sports that are genetically different will retain the odd growth pattern even when grafted or propagated from rooted cuttings. The growth may be twisted or congested and compact, variegated or an unusual shade or tint. From a horticultural standpoint, the brooms present opportunities for introducing new varieties.

If you keep your eyes peeled when looking at various plants, especially way up in the tops of evergreen conifers, you will undoubtedly come across some strange growth, like a flat stem on a willow or maple, or curly twigs and branches, or the most common, the familiar shaving-brush-shaped witches'-broom. You may find one as you walk up and down the streets of your town, or even in a nursery among the plants in the rows. The unusual part of the plant can be removed and rooted or, most often, grafted to the understock of a seedling of the parent species. It is possible that the coniferous brooms may bear cones, and the seeds produce yet more

GOOD THINGS IN SMALL PACKAGES

It may seem logical that given a choice between a young 3- to 4-foot-tall deciduous tree and an older 7- to 8-foot-tall one, planting the taller one will save time and produce faster results; but that isn't always the case.

While waiting for a *Franklinia alatamaha* tree I'd ordered from a mail-order nursery to arrive, I came across the same species in a nursery. I bought the nursery tree, and when the mail-order species arrived I planted them 10 feet apart. The one that came in the mail was 2 feet tall, and the nursery species was 6 feet. After seven years, the small mail-order tree was 7 feet tall, and the nursery tree about 4 feet tall, having died back during cold winters. For the sake of full disclosure, this Georgia native may not be reliably hardy in my zone. And I do not know the provenance—where the trees were propagated and grown. But the smaller tree established itself in its new digs quickly, and its new supple branches withstood cold and snow. One experience with two trees means little, but through the years I've found that if the choice is between a ten-year-old tree and a five-year-old tree, the younger one will often catch up and even overtake the larger one.

The smaller trees have probably been raised in beds or pots, and most likely shifted from one spot in the nursery to another. Small trees may also be sold dormant and "bareroot" from mail-order sources. These trees are dug out of the ground or unpotted after their leaves fall, and their roots are washed clean of soil. They may be sold right away in the autumn or refrigerated to hold for shipping in early spring.

Taller trees are often grown in sunny fields with irrigation, like a crop, to a uniform size, then sent to market and priced by the diameter of the trunk, or by height. These field-grown trees usually have straight trunks and firm, sun-baked bark. The branches have been pruned to maintain size and space between the trees in the nursery rows. The larger trees may be sold in containers, but more often in cold climates, they are dug out of the ground and their roots and soil (root ball) wrapped in burlap. These excavated trees are referred to as "balled-and-burlapped," or "B&B." When a young B&B tree is dug with a mechanical spade, up to 90 percent of its roots may be lost, but it survives nonetheless. However, when these taller B&B trees are planted in their permanent homes, they typically spend the first two or three years putting energy into making new roots rather than growing skyward. The tough bark, hardened from the wind and sun of the nursery rows, must also adjust to the new environment and soften to allow for expansion.

All of the burlap, plastic, wire baskets, and twine should be removed at planting time. The root flare, the place on the trunk where it begins to widen and meet the roots, must be located. Unfortunately, the flare may be buried in soil on B&B trees. In such cases, the soil should be cleaned away and the tree planted with the flare just above soil level. Watering deeply and frequently in the first few weeks after any tree transplanting, and if the weather gets hot, is the most important thing to do.

The smaller, bare-root or pot-grown trees seem to take off their first spring after being planted. If the small containerized tree is *not* pot-bound with constricted roots, it may put on prodigious new growth the first growing season after planting. Pot-bound trees should

be avoided, if possible. If you end up with a tree that is pot-bound, tease the roots free, or score the winding roots with vertical cuts made with a sharp knife in a few places around the ball before planting.

Why would anyone buy a pot-bound tree? Do you really have to ask? "It was the only one of that variety in the nursery, and I just had to have it," I'd say, congested roots and all.

OPPOSITE: *Franklinia alatamaha* flower and fall foliage. LEFT: *Cornus kousa* 'Wolf Eyes', balled and burlapped.

variations, but that isn't reliable or likely. If you find a broom, make a note of where it is and take a photo. You may find someone who is interested in propagating the broom.

I also like to look for plants with color variations, such as one seedling within a batch that looks a little different. Common changes could include variegation or reddish-colored leaves. Red is often caused by *anthocyanins*—pigments in plant tissues, which among other attributes, such as flower color and attraction to pollinators, may help defend leaves from cold. The effect of a reddish pigment can be seen in many evergreens that take on a purple to brown tinge in winter.

Besides color variations or changes in growth habit, different leaf shapes may develop as well. For instance, I love the fir *Abies koreana* 'Horstmann's Silberlocke', which appears pure silver. The bottom of the needles of many evergreens has a glaucous coating of wax or powder that keeps moisture in the needles and also reflects light and heat in summer. This Korean fir's needles curl around, exposing their silvery undersides, a stunning effect in any garden.

SHORT LIST

When I came to the island in New Jersey, there were several mature unusual trees here. Although I haven't been able to find out precisely who planted them, I have this imagined vision of itinerant bare-root tree salesmen driving their horse-and-buggies up and down the country roads shouting, "Trees for sale. Get your latest new Japanese trees for sale." I suppose it is possible, for several of these trees are Japanese, and they are unquestionably old.

Three 70-foot-tall conifers were here among the Japanese maples, and I did not

ABOVE, LEFT TO RIGHT:
Unusual witches'-brooms collected from needle-leaved conifers are often dwarfs. Dwarfs are usually slow-growing and smaller at maturity, but not tiny or miniature. Miniature evergreens are excellent candidates for planting in hypertufa troughs.

The needles of the selection of Korean fir (*Abies koreana* 'Horstmann's Silberlocke') roll up to reveal the waxy or glaucous undersides.

Dwarf evergreens at the Benenson Ornamental Conifers collection of the New York Botanical Garden.

ABOVE: In order to grow more trees and for the sake of design, I have selected narrow-growing columnar specimens, such as seven *Acer saccharum* 'Newton Sentry' sugar maples. This tree was originally discovered in the cemetery at Newton, Massachusetts, by nurseryman F. L. Temple in 1885.

ABOVE RIGHT: A few years later, 'Temple's Upright' was found. Also called 'Monumentale', this tree, which is not as narrow as 'Newton Sentry', looks as if it has been pruned and holds its leaves several weeks longer.

recognize them. Ultimately, when John Trexler, the director of Tower Hill Botanic Garden in Boylston, Massachusetts, was touring the property, he told me what they were. "Look at the silver Xs and Ys on the back of the leaves," he told me, and sure enough, they were there. "That's how you can recognize *Chamaecyparis pisifera*." I know this plant, but not from having seen the species. I had seen only dwarf versions that were little buns and spheres, thread-leaf gold versions and others between 5 inches and 10 feet tall.

Dwarf means small, compact, but also slow growing. I have seen "mature" versions of dwarf evergreen conifers that have reached the grand height of 15 feet at 100 years of age. But compared with their full-size counterparts at that age (70 to 130 feet tall) the plants are, indeed, small. There are also conifers that are practically automatic bonsai called miniature dwarf evergreens, shrubs that are super-tiny.

For small plantings and rock gardens, dwarf evergreens can be useful, especially when planted in containers, such as stone sinks or concrete or hypertufa troughs. I can imagine walking through a tiny forest, and stopping to rake the tiny gravel path with a comb. Dwarf plants allow gardeners, even those with small planting spaces, to grow trees, as long as there is plenty of sunlight. But bear in mind that "dwarf" often means slow and compact, and not necessarily permanently miniature. Some of these shrubs will in time—perhaps 20 or 30 years—outgrow their digs.

THE STRAIGHT AND NARROW

Growing dwarf trees and shrubs is one way to get more structure into smaller spaces. Another way to squeeze more into less space is by selecting varieties of trees that grow up instead of out and wide. I love the way these trees look, and I am

TOP: The already narrow tulip tree, farm-raised for telephone poles, also comes in a more narrow version, *Liriodendron tulipfera* 'Fastigiatum'.

ABOVE: There are many broadleaf and needle evergreen shrubs and trees that are also columnar, such as this variety of Japanese holly (*Ilex crenata* 'Sky Pencil').

glad they cast so little shade that other plants can grow around them. Of course, an added bonus, for me, is that these tall and skinny trees leave more room in the garden for collecting more plants in less space.

Trees with "apical dominance," such as the tulip tree and the English oak, continue to grow vertically, adding new wood to their ascending leader, in an *excurrent* manner. (Trees with vase shapes and spreading crowns have *decurrent* habits of growth.) There are selections of many tree species that have even narrower profiles, and some that are nearly cylinders. The words *fastigiate* and *columnar* are often used interchangeably to describe these very narrow-growing plants. More precisely, a fastigiate tree has a silhouette somewhat like a candle flame, while a columnar specimen has a more slender shape, like a pillar.

I have a kind of life list of plants I've seen or read about that I want someday to grow. Among these plant-lust candidates are the slender, columnar varieties. I searched for a variety of sugar maple, *Acer saccharum* 'Newton Sentry', for over a decade—long before I even had a place to grow one. This plant was propagated from a tree growing by the entrance to the Newton Cemetery in Newton, Massachusetts, by F. L. Temple, a Cambridge nurseryman. He took cuttings and introduced the plant in 1885.

After learning about the special trees that already grew on the land in New Jersey, and realizing that they stood in a somewhat rough circle roughly 130 feet in diameter, it seemed natural to accentuate this feature. Clearing brush from the center of the circle came next, and mowing the weeds, which encouraged various grass varieties to regain their dominance in what became my version of lawn—the cropped meadow. My idea was to plant about seven 'Newton Sentry' trees in a kind of elevated hedge, a scrim of maple "soldiers" in a second arc to accentuate the shape of the circle.

Sugar maples are famous for their brilliant color, but in the cool, humid valley, none of the local trees are very spectacular, and 'Newton Sentry' (syn. 'Columnare') turns a tame yellow. There are other columnar varieties of this maple, including 'Temple's Upright', also from F. L. Temple. That tree grows wider than 'Newton Sentry' and has a more uniform shape, almost as if it was pruned, and it holds its leaves much longer in the fall. Specimens of these two narrow maples can be seen at the Cornell Plantations Arboretum in Ithaca, New York, and one of the original 'Temple's Upright' grows at the Arnold Arboretum in Jamaica Plain, Massachusetts, where it is some 60 feet tall and 17 feet wide at 100 years of age.

Quercus palustris 'Green Pillar' is a columnar pin oak with superb scarlet to red foliage in autumn. I grow a very narrow *Liquidambar styraciflua* (a sweetgum, provisionally called 'Shadow Columnar Form') and a fastigiate *Liriodendron tulpifera* 'Fastigiatum' (a more slender version of the already narrow tulip poplar—the species grown for telephone poles).

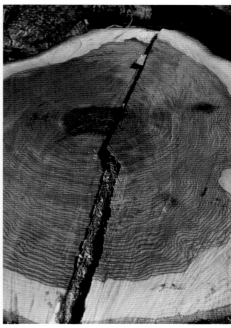

ABOVE: In the late 1930s, Fraser fir trees in the Great Smoky Mountains National Park were attacked by an adelgid that continues to kill mature trees. Like so many other living beings, trees are threatened by development, invasive species, diseases due to the stresses of global warming, islandization, etc. In years past, a blight destroyed nearly all the chestnut trees in North America. There is Dutch elm disease; hemlock's wooly adelgid; the Asian longhorn beetle; and other threats.

ABOVE RIGHT: Humans probably destroy the most trees, like this one cut down in Brooklyn, New York, by a man who campaigned for the city's assistance in removing a "messy" 100-year-old oak.

LOSSES

If trapped aboard a botanical *Titanic,* I know which plants I'd save first: trees. They have all the qualities that I value most in a plant, including age. In my plant hierarchy, longevity makes trees the most valuable.

The greatest threat to trees is not pests such as the gypsy moth, or Dutch elm disease, or the chestnut blight that wiped out every mature member of the woody plant. I have seen the enemy, and it is us. Loss of habitat is the number one threat to trees. But global climate change is also having an impact, with insects that are normally reduced in numbers during rough winters sailing through recent mild ones, and trees suffering from summer heat as well. A stressed tree is a pest magnet. I was in Quebec province several years ago and saw entire mountains that had turned brown with spruce trees decimated by insects in numbers not seen in colder years.

Sometimes people who should know better just don't. In 1964 a young geographer searching for evidence of Ice Age glaciers in Nevada came upon a stand of bristlecone pines growing at the timberline. He and his fellow students began taking core samples, inserting a narrow tubular drill that removes a section of wood to reveal the annual growth rings, which can be used to determine the age of the tree. But their only sampling tool broke. The end of the season was approaching, so instead of coming back with a new tool, they asked for and received permission from the U.S. Forest Service to cut down a tree and count the rings.

The geographer cut down a live tree, and when the growth rings were counted, it turned out that the pine had been 4,950 years old. It was the oldest known tree on Earth, and in fact the oldest living thing on Earth. And then it was dead.

Thousands of years ago, deforestation led to the desertification of the Fertile Crescent in the Middle East, and later, the New World counterpart in Central America suffered the same fate. Unfortunately, not much has been learned or changed since then. The loss of forested areas around the world in 2005 was put at a rate of 5 acres every hour of every day, according to the Food and Agriculture Organization of the United Nations. Seventy-five million acres of the world's forests are lost each year, including 15 million acres of old-growth forests.

When Columbus landed in what he thought was India, he stepped onto the island of Hispaniola. Today the western half of the island is known as Haiti; the eastern half, the Dominican Republic. More than 90 percent of Haiti has been stripped of trees felled for firewood and construction. The Dominican Republic, in contrast, has retained much of its tree-covered land. A storm in 2004 provided proof of the possible impact of deforestation. Torrential rains caused mudslides on the Haitian side, wiping out villages and killing thousands of people. The damage to the Dominican Republic, with its greater tree cover, was much less severe. When trees are present, the force of the rain is softened by tree leaves. Water trickles down the trunk and into the soil, which is made more porous by the tree's roots.

In poor countries, the number-one cause of premature death is not virus or war, it is the lack of safe drinking water. Without trees, excess surface water causes flooding, sewage overflows, and drinking-water supplies are contaminated. The flood of my property on April 16, 2007, from a nor'easter was the worst I'd seen in 12 years' gardening there. The island became the river, and whitecaps flowed across what was the cropped meadow in the center of the circle of trees. I know trees sometimes have to be cut down, but there are no restrictions on cutting trees on private property in my area. Development upriver from my home combined with global warming has led to worse and worse floods over the years.

In 1977, Wangari Maathai founded the Green Belt Movement (GBM) to combat rapid, commercially driven deforestation in her country, Kenya. According to Professor Wangari, the first person to be awarded a Nobel Peace Prize for environmental activism, the only solution to the rapid climate change we are experiencing is to plant trees. "It takes nothing to plant a tree," she said; "everyone can plant a tree." By 2005, some 30 million new trees were growing as a result of GBM's efforts.

GAINS

One neighbor in Brooklyn says he hates trees, because "they are messy." It is true; trees drop leaves. But this urbanite, who wants all trees cut down, doesn't have a clue that he would probably die without trees. The town of Old Westbury, New York, has an ordinance requiring people who take down a tree, even on their own property, to plant another one. I'm all for that kind of legislation, and I would go even further. I'd like to see municipalities require permits for the removal of any

RESURRECTION

When a deciduous tree or shrub fails to leaf out at the expected time, how does one know if it is alive? Gently scrape away a little bark on a stem of last year's growth. If the bark does not slip easily, and harder scratching reveals dry brown wood, it's curtains. But if when you gently scratch the bark it easily slips away to reveal green beneath, the plant is alive, and there *are* a few things that can be done to wake up an ailing shrub or tree.

When a plant is damaged in nature, a branch broken in a storm or a twig munched by a passing herbivore, hormones are sent to dormant buds just below the injury, telling undifferentiated cells to grow and replace whatever is needed. These cells can become leaves, branches, a new leader (the vertical growth of a tree), or even roots.

If the tips of last year's growth are dry and snap when I bend them, or the bark does not slip at the ends of the branches but does closer to the center of the plant, I prune back to live, green tissue. The light pruning, like physiological damage, tells the buds to wake up.

In general, you want branches to grow outward, not inward toward one another where they will block light and air and at times cross and scrape each other. You can encourage the direction of a branch by pruning just above an outward-facing bud.

An ailing plant should never be overfed or overwatered. But desperate times call for desperate measures, even the application of a vitamin-based botanical defibrillator. I have found that applying a liquid preparation containing vitamin B can help. These tonics are available from garden centers and some mail-order catalogs. Follow the recommended rates on the packages. With all products for the garden, it is important not to imagine that if a little bit is good, a little more will be better.

All gardeners have killed a plant or two. Believe me, you are not the first person to have presided over or contributed to a plant's demise. Along with the period of mourning comes analysis; I try to learn something from every loss. And, when it's time to remove a formerly treasured plant, I know that it will still contribute to the garden: vegetable matter can be recycled—ashes to ashes, chippings to compost.

OPPOSITE, CLOCKWISE FROM TOP LEFT: The vase shape is maintained by pruning (*Physocarpus opulifolius* 'Dart's Gold). Prune to outfacing leaf bud. Late new growth of *Cercis canadensis* 'Forest Pansy' dies back in winter, so prune tips back to live growth. Life can be determined when green is found under scratched bark.

tree larger than 2 feet in diameter (measured 1 foot above the ground). If a removal is found to be arbitrary following the inspection by a volunteer arboriculturist, then permission could be denied.

Maybe the government should put a value on doing good things for trees. How about tax deductions for exceeding the average pounds of oxygen produced? Or clean-water credits?

Well, there is always hope.

I write books like this one, and I hope my single voice makes a difference. When someone asks me what impact a lone voice can possibly make, I like to ask him or her, "Have you ever tried to sleep in a room with a single mosquito?" One human being can make a difference in a neighborhood, a town, a county, a state, maybe more, and certainly in the garden. We can choose organic options whenever possible, make compost, and use coir instead of ecologically suspect peat moss, a product that is harder to avoid than refined sugar. We can give local native species a safe haven, and plant more as they lose their habitats to development and browsing deer.

There is hopeful news. At last, "Green" is becoming chic.

Even if it is not law in your area, just make a pact with yourself to plant a tree for every one you have to remove, or the electric company or county road workers remove. The day before the flood of 2007, I planted 12 local birch trees grown from seedlings. Four were *B. papyrifera* (canoe or paper birch), and eight were *Betual lenta* (sweet birch), the source of birch beer. The tallest one was nearly 12 feet. After the deluge, I managed to find all but two. Three of them were still in the ground, on higher spots where I set them. Of the eight placed in lower areas, two were still planted. A couple were stuck in some shrubs, and two more were caught in the deer fence, lying horizontal on the ground. I found the tallest one a week later, up in a tree, but I planted it and it lived.

Ten saplings will help in the future if, or when, the property floods again. For dozens of reasons, trees are the most important living investment one can make, one that will pay dividends right away as well as into the next generation, and the generation after that. I am a gardener, not a farmer. But I do have a crop of choice, and it is trees. There's nothing like going out to the trees in your own backyard, and picking and biting into a nice, crisp gallon of fresh air.

RIGHT: Young local birch trees planted in a woodland garden.

OPPOSITE: In the early 1940s, a fossil was found of an ancient deciduous conifer. Shortly thereafter, these trees were discovered alive and thriving in China. In the 1950s, seedlings were distributed to institutions and influential private gardeners, and these trees can be seen around the country today at places such as the Morris Arboretum of the University of Pennsylvania in Philadelphia. These trees grew in both Asia and North America 30 million years ago—does that make *Metasequoia glyptostroboides* a native plant?

THE PATH AHEAD

We hear a lot about "plant blindness" these days. According to Dr. Peter H. Raven, director of the Missouri Botanical Garden, most Americans barely notice plants and can rarely identify them. For example, if people are shown an illustration of three elk in a woodland and asked what they see, the response is usually "three elk grazing." If a bird is added to the picture, people might say that it is an image of elk grazing under the watchful eye of a woodpecker, or blue jay or cardinal. Someone might mention that the elk were standing in a forest, but that's about it.

As Dr. Raven explains it, very few of us would note that this is a picture of "a classic temperate mix of maple, birch, and beech trees, and here's a spectacular basswood and, whoa, an American elm that shows no sign of fungal infestation and, oh yeah, three elk and a blue jay. Animals are much more vivid to the average person than plants are. Some people aren't even sure that plants are alive."

I've seen boys attacking a sapling on the streets of Brooklyn with a stick in an innocent game of swordplay—more than once. But I know that any of those kids would not think of hitting the tree if he had planted it himself, if he knew it was actually alive.

A BRAVE NEW WORLD

Soon after I came to this picturesque place where I live and garden in New Jersey, I discovered postcards on eBay that featured photographs of the property. I began to collect these vintage homages to the local landscape, as well as those featuring photos of the surrounding area, taken from my property.

There is one card postmarked 1905 that is special to me, not only for the image of the river and the little house but also for the note written on the back. A young girl wrote, "Papa, This is the place where you used to fish." She goes on recording the plants in the area. "There are *Clethra* here, and *Ilex* on the riverbank," she noted.

ABOVE: A 1905 postcard shows a bridge leading to the island where my garden grows. On the back, a young woman describes the plants she saw when she "botanized" in this area.

ABOVE RIGHT: In the 19th century, botanizing was a popular hobby. People would take samples, make drawings, and write descriptions of plants they encountered.

OPPOSITE, TOP TO BOTTOM: The young woman wrote about fragrant sweet pepperbush, described as *Clethra alnifolia*. A variegated modern selection, 'Creel's Calico', has leaves splashed with white.

Computer-savvy children could compare plants with kids around the world. Japanese maple species *Acer tegmentosum* with striped bark, for example.

A. pennsylvanicum is my local striped bark maple.

PRECEDING PAGE: *Opuntia* hardy cactus.

The pursuit of botany was all the rage in the 19th and early 20th centuries. Men, women, and children joined in, hunting for plants, armed with a small hand lens and a book or two to help identify the plants they found. They recorded the genus and species of trees and collected flowers and leaves, placing them carefully in tin boxes called *vascula*, to press and mount when they got home.

As the interest in gardening among the middle class grew, it was considered healthful to be outdoors in the fresh air, exercise, and enhance one's knowledge of the local flora. Botany was even considered a form of devotion, since natural theology—studying the Creator's handiwork—was proof of his goodness. Flower arranging and flower painting were acceptable pastimes for educated young ladies, and botany was an appropriate scientific endeavor, since unlike zoology, in which animals would have to be killed and dissected (both unladylike activities), plants could be picked and pressed for specimen records. (And in focusing on plants, there was less likelihood that women or children would inadvertently witness animal procreation.) Botanizing was also a way to socialize with people who shared a common interest, and a discreet way to meet members of the opposite sex.

The fear of contamination is perhaps even stronger today, but it is concern for the physical body, not the mind, that keeps people from exploring the natural world. I'm sure you've observed children—already closer to the ground than most adults—squat down to examine a busy ant. When I see a baby locked in a curious stare with a foraging insect, or touching the earth and feeling moist soil, I am filled with hope. Invariably, however, the baby's mother sweeps into the scene to whisk away her little innocent for a full body wipe-down with a germicidal towelette plucked from a plastic canister. Recent research suggests that the rise in asthma and allergies such as the one for the lowly peanut may be caused by not being exposed to, and developing antibodies for, certain things in the environment.

I'm not certain how we've gotten so far away from the wonder and awe our ancestors had for the world around them, but I think we owe it to ourselves and future generations to "inoculate" everyone who visits our gardens with a love of the natural world—children of all ages. If you have a garden, then you have an opportunity right outside your door. Take your child or grandchild by the hand and go outside. Turn over a rock and see what's living there. Learn together the names of what you find; discover a little creature's role in the life of the soil. Introduce the next generation to the tiny universe that exists in your very own backyard.

calling all botanophiles

I encourage you to reach out to your children and establish a new family tradition: a weekly "field trip" into the garden, the woods, the arroyos, the park—with magnifying glass and digital camera in hand. Encourage kids to draw the plants they see. And let the Internet help as one of your "field guides" for identifying the wildflowers, creatures you happen upon, or the mysterious animal prints in the snow. Perhaps you and your child could create a scrapbook, or even a "blog" of the "Smith Family's Field Adventures," and encourage friends and family to post comparison photos and scans of what they find in their backyard.

I can see it now: pen pals exchanging natural history notes from their neck of the woods: "Do you grow sunflowers in Singapore?" "Do you plant tulips in Turkey?"

Keep a tree journal, and identify all the trees on your property, around the neighborhood, and in botanical gardens, parks, and preserves. And just as birdwatchers keep a life list of sighted and identified bird species, you and your family can keep a running list of wildflowers.

Planting a tree together can be a wonderful way of celebrating a special occasion, even if that occasion is simply a sunny, mild Saturday. The tree can be the child's special plant to care for, and he or she can grow right along with it. Children (even if they are in their thirties) take a great deal of pride in showing visitors their trees. And a kid who knows a tree personally will rarely become the one who hits a young tree with a stick.

lead the way

Until they are shooed away one too many times, kids love being with their favorite grown-up. And, since they are eager to mimic us, the easiest way to spark children's interest in the great outdoors is to take them outside with you. Of course, if you don't want your precious posy pulling the petals off of your precious posies, trampling seedlings, or "helping" by gathering up all your carefully placed plant labels, then you'll want to set some limits.

The best way to keep the kids from possibly creating havoc is to give them a plot of their own. A baby won't cultivate much, but you will know when and if a

NATURE'S CLASSROOM

As the environmentally conscious children of the 1960s and '70s began to have children of their own, many schools started to rediscover the educational value of gardens and vegetable patches. A horticulturist at Cornell University reports that in her county, three-quarters of the schools have gardens, and that "it brings the curriculum to life."

The Willow School, in Gladstone, New Jersey, integrates natural surroundings into instruction. The students eat lunch outside and routinely walk the paths to observe wildlife or to play in the garden. Every classroom has a door that leads outside.

It isn't all that hard to imagine what might interest a kid. There seems to be almost a genetic predisposition that induces toddlers to smell flowers. My neighbor Jody Hagler sniffed flowers before she was old enough to talk. Kids find plants appealing from the start, I think, and like to anthropomorphize them, so flowers with faces, such as pansies, are especially appealing. Children are attracted to teeny tiny things, and mammoth ones as well. Plant a giant annual sunflower as well as tiny tomatoes, like 'Sweet One Hundred', which can be eaten right off the vine (as long as you don't use inorganic pesticides).

Seek out plants that appeal to all of the senses, such as stiff waxy *Bergenia* leaves that make the sound "pig squeak" when rubbed between your fingers. Feel the felted covering of small hairs, indumentum, on the back of *Rhododendron yakusimanum* leaves and *Magnolia grandiflora*, or the lamb's ears, silken *Plectranthus argentea*, and wooly thyme.

Fragrant herbs will be popular, especially ones such as scented geraniums that you can rub and sniff. Scented blossoms like heliotrope, lilacs, roses, and even tiny alyssum are appealing. You may have to bend way down to sniff the tiny plants, but a kid is almost there already.

Plants that move, such as *Mimosa pudica*, the sensitive plant, which closes its leaves when it is touched or even blown on, will certainly be popular. Other legumes "pray" at night, folding up their leaves when the sun sets. Seedpods of touch-me-not impatiens explode when barely tapped. Snapdragon flowers can be picked and squeezed to make them "talk."

There are a host of other plants to entice a child, many of which are probably already growing in your garden. Of course, creating a "child's garden" may inspire another trip to the nursery; if you're anything like me, you'll take any excuse for a shopping excursion!

OPPOSITE, CLOCKWISE FROM TOP LEFT: Water recycling pond at the Willow School. A friendly face seen in a pansy. Touch or blow on sensitive plants and the leaves fold. The untouched branches and leaves of *Mimosa pudica*, the sensitive plant.

ABOVE, LEFT TO RIGHT:
There are fascinating things to discover, like the fuzzy undersides of the evergreen southern magnolia (*M. grandiflora* 'Little Gem').

The *Plectranthus argentea* has silver plush leaves.

The eccentric rabbit's foot fern (*Davallia fejeensis*) has hairy rhizomes.

OPPOSITE, CLOCKWISE FROM TOP LEFT:
Rhododendron yakusimanum has a felted "indumentum" on the back of its leaves.

Six-year-old Jody Hagler examines autumn oak leaves.

The native *Aristilochia macrophylla* is the host plant for the pipevine swallowtail butterfly.

The 2-inch flowers resemble meerschaum pipes, which is the source of the common name Dutchman's-pipe.

toddler is ready to sow a sunflower seed, or plant a petunia, tomato, or tree seedling. You'd be surprised how those exploring hands will stop crushing your plants once children discover that doing that to one of their plants causes damage and loss. But losing a plant is not as bad as crushing a beginner's spirit. Accidents happen—to grown-ups, too. Lead gently, by example, and you'll cultivate a young gardener with a strong and generous heart.

Children love to hear stories, including tales of plants, which can also provide a great opportunity to teach about science, math, and even art. The chances are very good that many of the same things that appeal to you will captivate a child as well.

A colleague, Linda Romberger, once visited the garden with two of her children, Will, age eight, and Ileana, eleven. Their visit turned into an opportunity to test my contention that when you take kids outdoors and tell them a few of the sensational stories about plants and nature, you can lure them away from video games, perhaps even keep them from getting glued inside in the first place. Will and Ileana loved the showy lady's slipper orchids, were amazed by the scent of the lemon verbena, and could not get over the flowering cacti in the gravel garden.

When we came to the vines, they were enraptured by the story of Dutchman's-pipe. It's not easy to explain a meerschaum pipe to an eight-year-old, but I hooked them by sharing the fact that Dutchman's-pipe is the chosen food of a threatened butterfly species, the pipevine swallowtail. That year, one of the butterflies found the plant and laid her eggs, and I told them how excited I was to find the big larvae chewing holes in the plant's leaves. Will and Ileana listened intently. They were transfixed. They did not see the holes in the leaves as negative space, or damage, but as evidence of a great success. They saw the return of the pipevine swallowtail as a triumph in gardening, and so did I.

BIBLIOGRAPHY

Ackerman, Diane. *A Natural History of the Senses.* New York: Random House, Inc., 1990.

Brickell, C., and J. Zuk, Editors-in-Chief. *The American Horticultural Society A–Z Encyclopedia of Garden Plants.* New York: DK Publishing, 1996.

Burr, Chandler. *The Emperor of Scent: A Story of Perfume, Obsession, and the Last Mystery of the Sense.* New York: Random House, 2004.

Darke, Rick. *The Color Encyclopedia of Ornamental Grasses: Sedges, Rushes, Restios, Cat-tails, and Selected Bamboos.* Portland, Oregon, and Cambridge, England: Timber Press, 1999.

Dirr, Michael A. *Hydrangeas for American Gardens.* Portland, Oregon, and Cambridge, England: Timber Press, 2004.

Downing, A. J. *A Treatise on the Theory and Practice of Landscape Gardening, Adapted to North America: With a View to the Improvement of Country Residences.* New York: Dover Publications, 1991.

Greenaway, Kate. *The Language of Flowers.* London: Frederick Warne, 1900.

Griffiths, Mark. *The New Royal Horticultural Society Dictionary: Index of Garden Plants.* London: The Macmillan Press Ltd., and Portland, Oregon: Timber Press, 1994.

Hightshoe, Gary L. *Native Trees, Shrubs, and Vines for Urban and Rural America: A Planting Design Manual for Environmental Designers.* New York: Van Nostrand Reinhold; London: Chapman & Hall; Melbourne, Australia; Thomas Nelson Australia; and Ontario, Canada: Nelson Canada, 1988.

Hitchmough, Wendy. *Arts and Crafts Gardens.* London: Pavilion Books, and New York: Rizzoli International Publications, 1997.

Jean, Roger V. *Phyllotaxis: A Systemic Study in Plant Morphogenesis.* Cambridge, England: Cambridge University Press, 1995.

Lambourne, Lionel. *The Aesthetic Movement.* London: Phaidon Press, 1996.

Morris, Edwin T. *Fragrance: The Story of Perfume from Cleopatra to Chanel.* New York: Charles Scribner's Sons, 1984.

Musgrave, T., C. Gardner, and W. Musgrave. *The Plant Hunters: Two Hundred Years of Adventure and Discovery Around the World.* London: Ward Lock, 1999.

Neal, Bill. *Gardener's Latin: A Lexicon.* Chapel Hill, North Carolina: Algonquin Books, 1992.

Obrizok, Robert A. *A Garden of Conifers: Introduction and Selection Guide,* second edition, revised and expanded. Deer Park, Wisconsin: Capability's Books, 1994.

Pankhurst, Alex. *Who Does Your Garden Grow?* Colchester, England: Earl's Eye Publishing, 1992.

Phillips, H. Wayne. *Plants of the Lewis and Clark Expedition,* second printing. Missoula, Montana: Mountain Press Publishing Company, 2003.

Spencer, Robin. *The Aesthetic Movement.* London: Studio Vista Blue Star House, and New York: E. P. Dutton and Co., 1972.

Stuart, David C. *Dangerous Garden: The Quest for Plants to Change Our Lives.* London: Frances Lincoln, 2004.

Sumner, Judith. *The Natural History of Medicinal Plants.* Portland, Oregon, and Cambridge, England: Timber Press, 2000.

Wharton, Edith. *Italian Villas and Their Gardens.* New York: The Century Co., 1904.

Whittle, Tyler. *The Plant Hunters: Tales of the Botanist-Explorers Who Enriched Our Gardens.* New York: Lyons & Burford Publishers, 1997.

OPPOSITE: Autumn ginkgo leaves fallen on the pond in my garden.

SUGGESTED READING

Adams, Denise W. *Restoring American Gardens.* Portland, Oregon, and Cambridge, England: Timber Press, 2004.

Aslin, Elizabeth. *The Aesthetic Movement.* New York: Frederick A. Praeger, 1969.

Blackmore, S. *The Facts on File Dictionary of Botany.* New York: Facts on File, and United Kingdom: Penguin Books, 1984.

Chatto, Beth. *Beth Chatto's Gravel Garden.* London: Frances Lincoln, and New York: Penguin Putnam, 2000.

Darke, Rick. *In Harmony with Nature.* New York: Michael Friedman Publishing, 2000.

Hilton, Timothy. *The Preraphaelites.* London: Thames and Hudson, 1970.

Parry, Linda. *Textiles of the Arts & Crafts Movement.* London, Thames & Hudson, 2005.

Short, Philip. *The Pursuit of Plants.* Portland, Oregon, and Cambridge, England: Timber Press, 2003.

Tankard, Judith B. *Gardens of the Arts and Crafts Movement: Reality and Imagination.* New York: Harry N. Abrams, 2004.

Wood, Christopher. *The Pre-Raphaelites.* New York: The Viking Press, and Canada: Penguin Books Canada, 1981.

CREDITS

OPPOSITE: Good gardens reveal a guiding hand, as in the London plane tree allee at Greenwood Gardens in Short Hills, New Jersey.

INDEX

Corydalis spp., 67
cottage gardens, 51, 51, 180, 197
cowslip, 120, 120
crabapple, 98
cranberry, 94
crescent border, 13, 73, 75
crucifers, 156, 159, 160
Crystal Palace, 186, 190, 190
Cullina, Bill, 104
cultivar names, 45, 45
cup-and-saucer vine, 203, 205, 212
curare, 59
Cycas sp., 156
Cyclamen spp., 112–113, 113
Cypripedium spp., 104, 104

D

daffodil (Narcissus), 126–127, 127
Dahlia spp., 94
daisy family, 159, 159
dame's rocket, 160
dancing ladies, 170
dandelion, 113–114
Daphne spp., 120, 120, 170
darning needles and dragon flies, 250, 251
Darvill, Ben, 96
Datura (jimsonweed, thorn apple, locoweed), 141, 141
Davallia argentea (rabbit's foot fern), 278
Davidia involucrata (dove tree), 13
Da Vinci, Leonardo, 155, 159, 168, 168, 195
daylily, 87, 87, 93, 93
deer, 76, 156, 234–235, 236, 238, 238
deforestation, 267
Delphinium hybrids, 195, 238, 238, 241
Deutzia spp., 228, 233
devil's tongue, 147, 147
Dianthus sp., 206, 257
Dicentra spp. (bleeding heart), 67
Dicksonia antarctica (Tasmanian tree fern), 22
Digitalis spp. (foxglove), 73–79, 84
dinosaur kale, 159
dioecious plants, 93
divine proportion, 159–160
Doctrine of Signatures (Paracelsus), 52, 55
dogwood. See Cornus
doll's eyes, 60
Dominican Republic, 267
Donahue, Marcia, 145, 243
Douglas, David, 33, 35–36
dove tree, 13
Downing, Andrew Jackson, 177
dracaena, 75
Dracunculus vulgaris (dragon arum, voodoo lily), 147
dragonflies and darning needles, 250, 251
Dresser, Christopher, 201–202
Drummond, Robert, 22
Dutchman's pipe, 278, 278

E

Easter lily, 184
Echeveria hybrid, 172

Echinacea species and hybrids (purple coneflower), 81, 89, 89–90, 90
Echinops ritro (globe thistle), 153
Edelman, Edith, 172
elephant's ear, 147–148
Endeavour expedition, 18, 21, 22
enfleurage, 128
The English Flower Garden (Robinson), 180, 199
Ensete ventricosum (red banana), 30
Epimedium sp., 159
Epiphyllum spp., 100, 143, 143–144
Equisetum spp. (horsetail), 42
Eryngium spp. (sea holly), 106, 107
Eschscholzia californica (California poppy), 33
ethnobotany, 45
Eucalyptus regnans, 18
Eucomis 'Sparkling Burgundy' (purple pineapple lily), 244
Eupatorium (Joe Pye weed), 102, 102
European snowball, 225
evening and night-scented plants, 135, 138–144
Exochorda × macrantha (pearl bush), 228

F

Fabaceae, 168
Fairey, John, 35
false hellebore, 55
Fatshedera hybrids, 87, 87
Fibonacci, 159, 164, 164, 166, 168, 174
Ficus (fig), 45, 111, 111–112
filler plants and ground covers, 241–247
five-petaled plants, 156, 162
fleur-de-lis, 206, 207–208
flies and beetles, 98, 145, 147, 150, 191
Flintoff, Jerry, 75, 79
flooding, 267
flowering cherry, 201
flowering quince, 159
flowering raspberry, 159
food plants, 45, 47–49, 51
forsythia, 233
Fortune, Robert, 30, 33
four-o'clocks, 139
four-petaled plants (crucifers), 156, 159, 160
foxglove (Digitalis spp.), 73–79, 84
fragrance. See scent
Franklinia alatamaha, 260, 261
Fraser fir, 265
Fritillaria meleagris (checkered lily), 178, 202
frogs, 251, 253
fuchsia hybrids, 206

G

galls, 110, 111–112, 117
Gardenia spp., 4, 120
Garden in the Woods (New England Wild Flower Society), 10, 104
Gaudí, Antonio, 202

Gentiana andrewsii (bottle gentian), 243
genus names, 42
geophytes, 126
geranium, scented, 120, 120
Geranium spp., 94, 243, 245–246, 253, 253
Geum triflorum (prairie smoke), 10
Ginkgo biloba (maidenhair tree), 145, 256–257, 257, 281
Globba winitii (dancing ladies), 170
globe thistle (Echinops ritro), 153
gloriosa lily, 203, 205
The Glory of the Scientist (Linnaeus), 33
golden ragwort, 253
golden ratio (golden mean, golden rectangle, golden section), 9–10, 159–160, 163, 164, 164, 166, 168, 168, 171
golden spiral. See spirals and golden spirals
grape vine, 203, 205
gravel garden, 26, 26, 28, 170, 172, 174
Great Exhibition (1851), 186, 186, 190, 190
Great Smoky Mountains National Park, 265
Greenaway, Kate, 185
Green Belt Movement, 267
greenhouses, 28, 29
Greenwood Gardens, 204, 236, 283
ground covers and filler plants, 241–247
Guimard, Hector, 202
Gwynn, John, 253
gymnosperms, 109, 109

H

Hagler, Jill, 132
Hagler, Jody, 276, 278
Haiti, 267
Hakonechloa macra 'Aureola', 67, 235
Hamilton, Heidi, 243
Harper's Magazine, 64
Hassam, Childe, 179
Helenium autumnale (sneezeweed), 162, 166
Helianthus spp. (sunflower), 161–162, 164, 164, 166, 166
Heliopsis 'Loraine Sunshine', 166
Helleborus spp. (hellebore), 90, 90, 93, 93, 243, 245
Hemerocallis spp. (daylily), 87, 87, 93, 93
hens-and-chicks (Sempervivum), 172–173, 173, 174
herb gardens, 47–49, 51
heroin, 63, 64
Hesperis matronalis (dame's rocket), 160
heterosis, 93, 134
Heucherella hybrids, 84, 84
Hibiscus syriacus 'Diana' (Rose of Sharon), 215
Hinkley, Dan, 232
Hoffmann, Josef, 202
hollyhocks, 197
honeybees, 94, 96, 97
horsetail, 42

Horta, Victor, 202, 202
Hosta, 170, 238
H. 'Francis Williams', 285
H. plantaginea, 170
H. sieboldiana, 36, 41, 241, 244
hummingbirds, 98, 98
Hunt, William Holman, 183–184
Hyacinthus orientalis (hyacinths), 127
hybrids and hybridizing, 84–93
Hydrangea spp., 41, 41, 42, 218, 218–221, 219

I

Ilex crenata 'Sky Pencil' (Japanese holly), 264
Ilex species and hybrids, 93, 93
indumentum, 276, 278
ink (oak gall ink), 110, 117
insect pollination, 94–100, 102, 145, 147, 150, 191
International Code of Nomenclature for Cultivated Plants, 42
International Exhibition (1862), 201, 201–202, 202
Iris spp., 35, 98, 207–211
irrigation, 48, 48, 49
Islamic gardens, 48, 49
Italian Villas and Their Gardens (Wharton), 177, 179
ivy, 60, 204

J

jack-in-the-pulpit, 17, 18, 253
Japan, 36, 41, 198, 201, 201–202, 202
Japanese anemone, 206
Japanese maple, 250, 274
Japanese snowball, 225, 225
Jekyll, Gertrude, 199, 199, 201
Jensen, Jens, 177–178, 178
jimsonweed, 141, 141
Joe Pye weed, 102, 102
Josephine, empress of France, 178, 179

K

Kenya reforestation project, 267
Kepler, Johannes, 166
Kerr, William, 22, 22
Kerria japonica, 22
Kew Gardens, 22, 191
Kingdon-Ward, Frank, 68
Klimt, Gustav, 202
Kniphofia spp., 168, 170
knot gardens, 51, 51
Kolkwitzia amabilis (beautybush), 228
Korean fir, 262, 262

L

Labiatae, 159, 159
lamp shades, 21, 21
The Land of the Blue Poppy (Kingdon-Ward), 68
Language of Flowers (Greenaway), 185
Latin names. See names of plants
lavender, 120, 120